Edward Lewes Cutts

Augustine of Canterbury

Edward Lewes Cutts

Augustine of Canterbury

ISBN/EAN: 9783743313064

Manufactured in Europe, USA, Canada, Australia, Japa

Cover: Foto ©ninafisch / pixelio.de

Manufactured and distributed by brebook publishing software (www.brebook.com)

Edward Lewes Cutts

Augustine of Canterbury

AUGUSTINE OF CANTERBURY

BY

EDWARD L. CUTTS, D.D.

BOSTON AND NEW YORK
HOUGHTON, MIFFLIN AND COMPANY
The Riverside Press, Cambridge
1895

CONTENTS

CHAP.		PAGE
	CHRONOLOGICAL TABLE	vii
	PEDIGREE OF THE KINGS OF KENT	x
	PEDIGREE OF THE FRANK KINGS	xi
	TABLE OF BISHOPS	xii
I.	THE ROME OF GREGORY THE GREAT . . .	1
II.	GREGORY THE GREAT	7
III.	THE YORKSHIRE BOYS IN THE ROMAN FORUM . .	15
IV.	THE DEPARTURE OF THE MISSION	21
V.	AT MARSEILLES	26
VI.	THE JOURNEY THROUGH FRANCE	33
VII.	ENGLAND IN 596 A.D.	42
VIII.	THE RECEPTION OF THE MISSION	50
IX.	THE SUCCESS OF THE WORK	57
X.	GREGORY'S INSTRUCTIONS	66
XI.	ESTABLISHMENT OF THE CHURCH IN CANTERBURY .	76
XII.	THE ARRIVAL OF THE SECOND BODY OF MISSIONERS .	86
XIII.	THE HISTORY OF THE PALL	94
XIV.	GREGORY'S LETTERS, TO AUGUSTINE ON HIS MIRACLES, AND TO ETHELBERT	101

CONTENTS

CHAP.		PAGE
XV.	THE BEGINNINGS OF THE LIBRARY OF THE ENGLISH CHURCH.	107
XVI.	THE OLD TEMPLES AND CHURCHES	111
XVII.	THE FOUNDATION OF THE MONASTERY OF SS. PETER AND PAUL	117
XVIII.	THE NEGOTIATION WITH THE BRITISH CHURCH	126
XIX.	THE ENDEAVOUR TO EXTEND THE CHURCH TO THE OTHER ENGLISH KINGDOMS	147
XX.	THE EPISCOPACY OF LAURENTIUS	152
XXI.	THE DEATH OF ETHELBERT; THE APOSTASY	157
XXII.	THE MISSION TO NORTHUMBRIA	161
XXIII.	PROGRESS OF THE WORK IN NORTHUMBRIA	168
XXIV.	THE EPISCOPATE OF HONORIUS	184
XXV.	THE KENTISH MONASTERIES	187
XXVI.	ARCHBISHOP THEODORE	196
	INDEX	205

CHRONOLOGICAL TABLE

In drawing up a Chronological Table for the reader's convenience, it is necessary to say that only some of the dates are certainly fixed, but these occur at intervals which form a skeleton table into which the other dates can be intercalated without fear of any considerable error.

The History of St. Augustine's Monastery, by William Thorn, a monk of that house in 1397, gives the following dates:— Augustine sent to England, 596; Baptism of Ethelbert, Pentecost, 597; Augustine consecrated, 16th November 597; Received the Pall, 601; Augustine died, 26th May 605; Ethelbert and Bertha kept Christmas at St. Augustine's, 605; Abbot Peter died, 607; Laurentius consecrated the Abbey Church, 613; and died, 614; Ethelbert died, 616; Justus died, 635; Honorius died, 643; Deusdedit died, 664; Theodore appointed to the bishopric, 670.

Thomas of Elmham, a monk of the same house, in 1412, prefixed an elaborate *Chronologia Augustinensis* to his *History of the Monastery*, from which the following dates are taken:— Arrival of Augustine, Baptism of Ethelbert, Foundation of the Monastery, all in 597; Peter made Abbot, 598; Pall sent, 603; Mellitus and Justus consecrated, 604; Death of Augustine, 26th May 605; Dedication of the Church by Laurence, 613; Death of Laurence, 619; Death of Mellitus, 625; Edwin of Northumbria baptized, 627; Death of Justus, 635; Death of Honorius, 653; Vacancy of eighteen months; Deusdedit elected, 655; Deusdedit died, 664; Vacancy; Theodore consecrated, 668; arrives in England, May 27, 669.

A.D.

586 or 587. Gregory undertakes a mission to England, and is recalled.
590. Gregory made Bishop of Rome.
596. Augustine leaves Rome for Britain in the spring; leaves the second time, July 23rd.
597. Augustine consecrated Bishop in autumn.
597. Baptism of the ten thousand at Christmas.
598. Laurence and Peter sent to Rome and return.
598.? Baptism of Ethelbert on Whitsunday.
601. Arrival from Rome of Abbot Mellitus and his company.
601. The Pall sent to Augustine.
603.? The Synod at Augustine's Oak.
604. Mellitus consecrated Bishop of East Saxons, and Justus of Rochester.
604. Laurence consecrated before April.
604. Death of Gregory, 12th March.
605.? Augustine died, May 26th; Laurence succeeded.
613. Monastery of SS. Peter and Paul consecrated.
616. Ethelbert died; succeeded by Eadbald.
617. Flight of Mellitus and Justus to France.
618. Return of Mellitus and Justus.
619.? Laurence died, succeeded by Mellitus.
624. Mellitus dies, April 24th, succeeded by Justus.
625. Paulinus consecrated, July 21st, for Northumbria.
627. Justus dies, succeeded after an interval by Honorius.
630. Monastery of Dover founded; Conversion of East Anglia by Bishop Felix.
633. Defeat and death of Edwin, King of Northumbria; return to Kent of Ethelburga and Paulinus.
633. Double monasteries of Folkestone and Lyminge founded.
635. Conversion of the West Saxons by Bishop Birinus.

A.D.
- 640. Eadbald dies, succeeded by Earconberht.
- 644. Paulinus dies at Rochester, succeeded by Ithamar.
- 653. Conversion of the East Saxons by Cedd.
- 653. Honorius dies; an interval of eighteen months.
- 655. Deusdedit consecrated.
- 664. King Earconbert and Bishop Deusdedit died the same day, July 14th; the former succeeded by Egbert; a vacancy in the see.
- 666.? Wigheard sent to Rome and dies there.
- 668. Theodore of Tarsus consecrated Archbishop of Canterbury.
- 669. The King gave Reculver to Bass the priest to build a minster there.

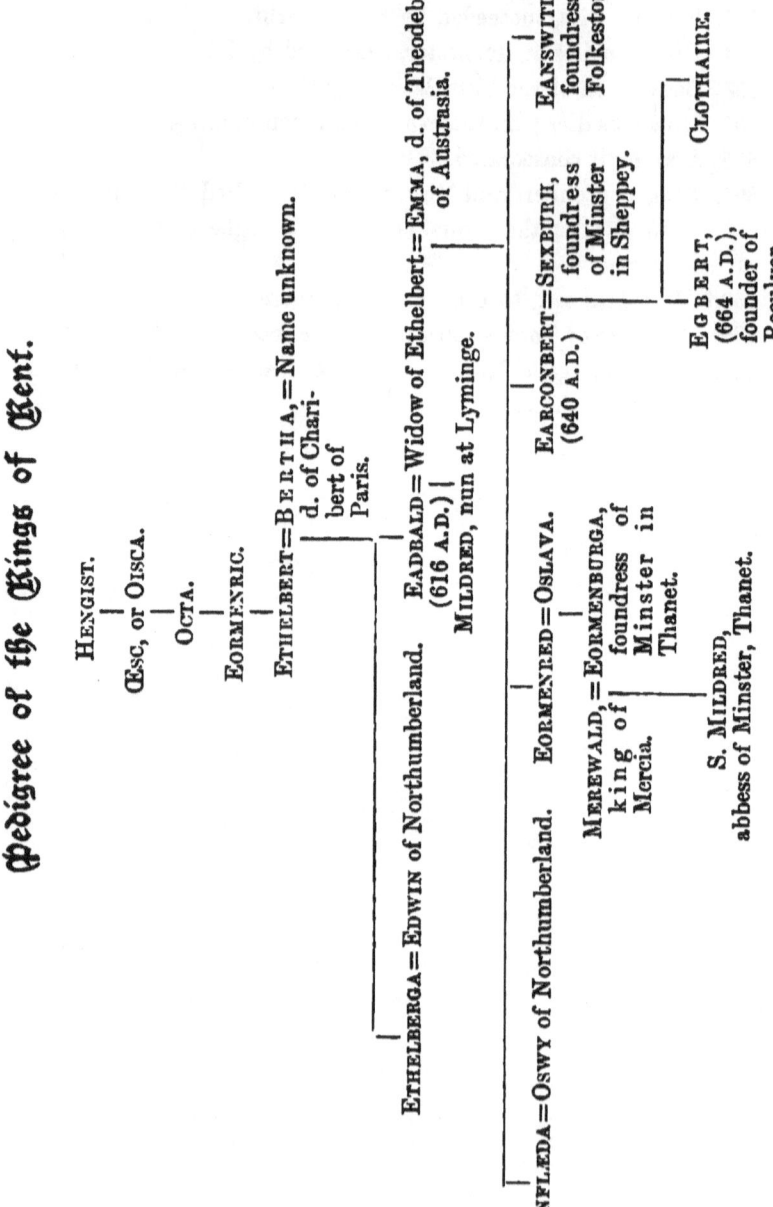

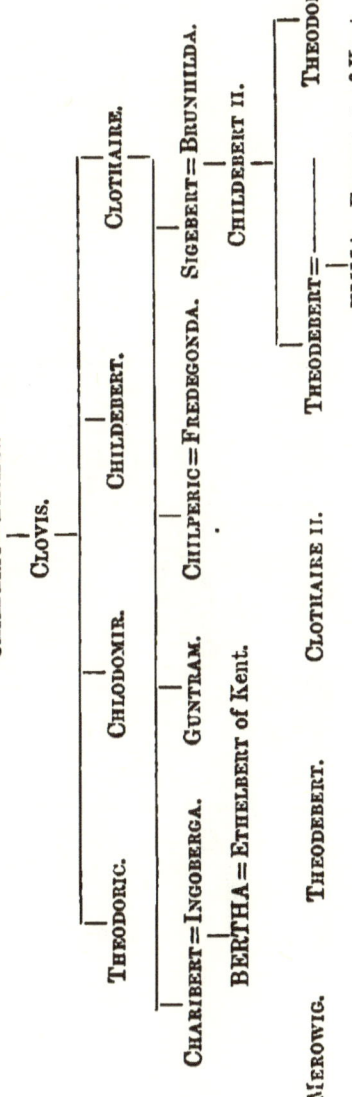

Bishops of the Period included in this Book.

Rochester.	East Saxons.	Northumbria.	East Anglia.	West Saxons.	Mercia.	South Saxons.
A.D.	A.D.	A.D.	A.D.	A.D.	A.D.	A.D.
Justus 604	Mellitus 604, abandoned his See 616					
Romanus 624		Paulinus 625, fled to Canterbury 635				
Paulinus 635		Aidan 637	Felix 630	Birinus 636		
Ithamar 644		Finan 651	Thomas 647 Boniface 652	Agilbert 650		
Damian 655	Cedd 654	Colman 661			Diuma 656 Ceollach 658 Trumenere 659	
	Wini 662	Tuda 664		Wini 662	Jaruman 662 Chadd 664	

AUGUSTINE OF CANTERBURY

CHAPTER I

THE ROME OF GREGORY THE GREAT

THE Rome of Gregory the Great was no longer the powerful and splendid city of the early Emperors with which we are most familiar. It had long since ceased to be the capital of the Empire. From the death of Gallienus (A.D. 260), with the short interval of seven years of the reigns of Tacitus and Probus (275–282 A.D.), the Emperors had practically ceased to reside in Rome; the defence of the Empire from the Barbarians required their presence nearer the frontiers, at the centre of military operations; and the camp was also the court and the centre of political administration.

When Diocletian divided and reorganised the Empire, he founded an Eastern capital at Nicomedia, on the eastern shore of the Propontis, which Constantine removed to Constantinople on the western shore of the Bosphorus. Milan was chosen as the capital of the Western Augustus. Both, with the concourse of people which public affairs and private interests and pleasures attract to a capital, grew into great cities, and were adorned with such splendid public buildings as became the dignity of the Empire.

While a new nobility, of the great officers of the army and of the household and of the provincial governors, was growing up at the new capitals, the great nobles of old Rome held themselves aloof from the courts of the imperial adventurers, and kept up the splendour and luxury of the ancient city out of the revenues of the vast estates acquired by their ancestors in all parts of the world which Roman arms had subdued.

This splendid luxury was rudely interrupted. Alaric with his Goths appeared before the gates of the city in 409 A.D., and was bought off with a great ransom. But he came again the following year and gave up the city to sack and plunder.

It was the nobles who suffered most; their wealth was the great prize at which the Barbarians aimed; their palaces were the first objects of the pillagers. Who shall tell the fate of a proud, luxurious aristocracy amidst the brutal horrors of a city given up to sack and pillage by a horde of Barbarians. Many were put to the sword; some were tortured to make them reveal the supposed hiding-place of their treasures; some disappeared under the ruins of their burnt palaces; some escaped to Africa and elsewhere; some perished under the hardships of their flight. Rome was left half consumed by fire and half depopulated. Its fate excited the horror and amazement of the civilised world. Half a century (455 A.D.) later, the Vandals under Genseric completed the plunder of the city. "The pillage lasted fourteen days and nights; all that yet remained of public or private wealth, of sacred or profane treasure," down to the bronze of the statues and the furniture of brass and copper, was carried away in the ships of the African conqueror. And yet a third time the soldiers of Ricimer, in 472 A.D., forced their way into the city, and indulged in unrestrained rapine and licence, in which the mob and the slaves of the city joined them. Rome thus ruined, fell into the condition of a place of second-rate importance.

When Theodoric the Ostrogoth made himself master of Italy, he took up his residence at Ravenna; but he visited Rome, was filled with admiration of the grandeur of its ancient monuments, and took pains to encourage its returning prosperity. After sixty years of subjection to the Gothic yoke, Belisarius rescued it (536 A.D.), and added it to the dominions of the Eastern Emperor.

Then came the invasion of the Lombards, who occupied the north, the south, and scattered portions of the middle of the country; leaving to the Eastern Emperor a tract of country between the Adriatic and the Apennines around Ravenna, and the three subordinate provinces of Rome, Venice, and Naples, isolated amidst the Lombard conquests, under the rule of the Exarch of Ravenna. During two hundred years this division continued under eighteen successive Exarchs. It was not till 755 A.D. that King Pepin gave his Lombard conquests of that year to the See of St. Peter, to be held as a fief of the Frankish kingdom; and not till the disruption of the Carolingian Empire, in the latter part of the ninth century, that the Pope, together with other feudatories, was able to hold his dominions as an independent prince. Our present concern is with Rome at the close of the sixth century, when it was still part of the Eastern Empire.

The Roman province extended along the coast from Civita Vecchia to Terracina, and inland to Ameria and Narni. During the period which we have reached—the close of the sixth century—the Duchy of Rome was in this condition: it was a dependency of the Exarchate of Ravenna, isolated amidst the Lombard conquests; ruled by the Exarch and his representative in Rome, but left to defend itself by its own diplomacy and force, in face of the hostile attitude of the Lombard Duke of Beneventum on the south. In 570-582, the clergy and Senate collected the remains of their ancient opulence, and sent an embassy to the Emperor Tiberius II., asking aid, and offering three thousand pounds of gold as their contribution to the cost of the expedition. The Emperor declared his inability to help them, and returned the money, advising the Romans either to buy peace from the Lombards with it, or to spend it in hiring the aid of the Franks. Rome had reached the lowest point of its depression. The influx of wealth from the revenues of the provinces had ceased; strangers no longer resorted to it for business or curiosity; large parts of the city were in ruins; the Campagna was falling into the condition of an unwholesome waste, from which it has never recovered. So great were the miseries of the time, as to produce in many minds the belief that the end of the world was at hand.

The Church of Rome had shared in the misfortunes

of the city. In the previous centuries, the See, endowed by the piety of wealthy devotees with estates in Italy and the provinces, and further enriched by continual offerings, was very wealthy. The legal recognition accorded by the Christian Emperors to the arbitration of bishops between disputants, and the deference paid to their intercession on behalf of accused persons, had placed the bishop virtually among the chief magistrates of the city; and the magistracy of Rome maintained some of the pretensions of the ancient Senate; the position of the Bishop of Rome had therefore been one of great wealth, dignity, and influence.

But the overthrow of the Empire and the ruin of Rome had dried up the chief sources of the wealth of the See, and, under the rule of Ostrogothic Kings and Eastern Emperors, it had lost much of its prestige. Both rulers had maintained the right of intervention in the appointment of bishops, and both had treated the bishops as their subjects. Theodoric had sent Bishop John to Constantinople, as his ambassador, to obtain for the Arians in the East that toleration which the Arians gave to the Orthodox in the West, and on his return had cast him into prison for the partial failure of his mission, where he shortly died (536 A.D.). Theodahat had sent Bishop Agapetus, as his ambassador, to avert a threatened attack. When Belisarius had conquered the city, he, or rather his wife Antonina, had summoned Bishop Sylverius to her chamber, rated him for treasonable correspondence with the besieging Goths, sent him off by sea to the East, and caused Vigilius to be elected in his place. Vigilius (545 A.D.) had been summoned to court by Justinian to give an account of himself, and had been detained there seven years, and died on his way homeward. The vacillation of Vigilius on the great theological dispute of the time had even sullied the reputation of the See for its soundness in the faith, and diminished its spiritual authority. In the time of his successor Pelagius, the rest of the Italian bishops withdrew from communion with Rome, and the province of Aquileia maintained its excommunication of Rome for nearly a century and a half. This was the Rome of Gregory the Great, and the scene of the opening of the present history.

CHAPTER II

GREGORY THE GREAT

GREGORY THE GREAT (Anicius Gregorius) is said to have descended from the Anician family. His grandfather was Bishop Felix III.; his father, Gordian, was the noblest of the Senate; his mother, Sylvia, illustrious for her piety, retired to a convent on her husband's death. Gregory entered into civil life, and attained the highest municipal office of prefect of the city. But at the age of thirty-five (about 575 A.D.) he fell under the influence of the prevalent ascetic enthusiasm, and entered what was technically called the "religious" life. He converted the house of his family on the Cælian Hill into a monastery dedicated to St. Andrew, and devoted the remainder of his patrimony to the founding of six monasteries in Sicily. Whether he adopted the rule which St. Benedict had drawn up for his monks fifty years before, is not stated by the contemporary authorities, and is disputed by the modern historians. Gregory was a great admirer of Benedict, and wrote his biography; but he was a man of so much originality of genius and self-reliance, so much in the habit of seeking to improve what he touched, that while he could hardly help taking the rule of Benedict in its broad outlines as a wise adaptation, on the whole, of the Eastern rule to

Western conditions, he would be very likely to modify it at his own discretion. It is a point of some importance, since Augustine, who was a man of routine, would be sure to introduce the rule of St. Andrew's of the Cælian Hill into the monasteries of Kent. It may be noted here that when Benedict Biscop founded his Northumbrian monasteries at Wearmouth and Jarrow, he did not adopt the Benedictine rule as a matter of course, but gave them an eclectic rule based upon his study of the most famous monasteries of Italy and Gaul.

The position and talents of Gregory were enough to ensure him an eminent position in the Church, as formerly in the civil service of his native city. It was the custom of the time for the great Patriarchs to maintain an agent (*Apocrisiarius*) at the court of the Emperor, to watch over the interests of their churches, and to transact the business frequently arising. Pelagius II. sent Gregory in 578 or 579 to Constantinople in this capacity, Tiberius II. being Emperor; and here he must have acquired, during the six years of his residence, a skill in diplomacy and a knowledge of men and affairs which would be useful in the political difficulties with which it was afterwards his lot to deal.

It is necessary to a right understanding of our history, to consider carefully the position of the Bishops of Italy and Gaul at this period. The early Christians, acting upon the precept of St. Paul not to go to law with one another before the heathen courts (1 Cor. vi. 1–6), had made a practice of referring their disputes to the arbitration of their bishops. The Christian Emperors had recognised the custom, and given legal force to the episcopal decisions. This had the effect of giving the bishops jurisdiction, and putting them among the chief magistrates of their cities. From a complaint of St. Augustine of Hippo, we learn that a considerable portion of the time of a bishop of that period was taken up with the fulfilment of these judicial functions. Again, the bishops exercised an independent but considerable influence over the ordinary action of the law. It was something like the devolution upon the bishops of the power which the tribunes of the people possessed in earlier times, to interpose between the people and the ordinary magistrates. The opinion of the time deemed it a proper exercise of the sacred function of a bishop to interpose on behalf of one whom he thought oppressed, and even to intervene on behalf of those who had been justly condemned, on the ground of their repentance. The bishop's house had the privilege of sanctuary, no one who had succeeded in obtaining a footing within its precincts could be arrested there; and even the bishop's person had the same privilege, a man who could lay hold of the bishop, even of the hem of his robe, was under this inviolable protection, and free from immediate molestation.

In the disruption of the Western Empire, the fate of the churches in those parts of the Continent of Europe, where the Goths and Franks won permanent settlements, was very different from the destruction with which the ruder tribes of Angles and Saxons overwhelmed the churches of the deserted province of Britain. There the conquerors settled in the fertile lands, and readily made terms with the cities, leaving them to continue their life under their own laws, administered by their own municipal magistrates. In the old times the Emperor had an official in each city to receive the imperial tribute and watch over the imperial interests; the Frank and Gothic kings replaced the Roman official by a Frank or Gothic count, who possessed the same powers, but naturally far less influence. Each city, therefore, with the surrounding territory—sometimes very extensive—which belonged to it, continued its civil and church life as a little self-governing republic.

In this civil and church life the bishop was the most wealthy, powerful, and influential person. The weight of his official position was frequently enhanced by personal circumstances. It was the custom for the churches to choose for their bishop some neighbouring person of distinction. A man of noble family and wealth, who had held high civil office, was the kind of man who seemed to them best fitted to occupy the highest place in the civil and ecclesiastical government of the city, to protect them from abuse of his office on the part of the Roman prefect or the Teutonic count, and to plead the cause of the city or of individual citizens, when occasion required, before the Emperor or King. Moreover, it was the custom for a bishop to spend his revenues upon the people, and to make large donations or bequests to his See, so that the interests of the people in many ways were engaged in the choice of the greatest of their neighbours for bishop, if his character were otherwise such as to qualify him for the highest ministry of the Church. Again, it was the custom of the time for the person chosen as bishop to profess a sense of utter unworthiness for the office, and to make a vehement resistance. This was met by a corresponding urgency; the more unwilling a man was, the better fitted he thereby proved himself to be. If he hid himself they sought him out, if he fled they fetched him back; the matter sometimes went so far that the man chosen by the Church was consecrated by a gentle force in spite of his protestations. On the whole, it was thought that the Church had a right to the services of the man upon whom the choice of the city fell; and when his resistance had sufficiently tested the reality and unanimity of the choice, the man felt it a duty to accept the office. Thus every great city in Italy, Gaul, and Spain at this period was virtually a republic, and the bishop was, by his office, wealth, and influence, the greatest man in it.

The position of the Bishop of Rome at this time was essentially the same as in the other cities, and had grown up in the same way; only Rome, though half ruined and half depopulated, was still greater than the other cities, and the bishop's position was proportionately grander. Moreover, the Bishop of Rome was a Patriarch of the Church, with relations with the other Patriarchs; he was the principal Metropolitan of Italy, and claimed a certain amount of authority over its bishops; he had influence in Gaul, and was beginning to assert a novel authority over its churches. These details will help us further to understand generally the Church life of the time of Gregory with which we are dealing, and particularly the next passage in the history.

When, on the death of Pelagius II. in 590 A.D., the unanimous voice of the clergy, Senate, and people of Rome nominated Gregory as Bishop, he protested against their choice, and wrote to the Emperor, begging him to refuse to confirm it; for the Emperors since Constantine had claimed and exercised at least a negative voice in the appointment to the Sees of the greatest cities. The prefect, however, withheld Gregory's letter, and substituted for it one of his own, in which he stated the desire of all classes of the people of Rome, and begged for the Emperor's confirmation of it. When the confirmation arrived, Gregory fled from the city; he was followed and brought back, and consecrated in September, 590 A.D.

This was the Rome and these the conditions of its civil and ecclesiastical organisation when Gregory was elected to its See. It was necessary to say thus much of Gregory, for he is a chief person in our present story. The mission to Kent was of Gregory's sending, and he kept his hand upon it. Augustine was his agent, and his merit is that he faithfully carried out his master's instructions. But we need not pursue the history of the great Pope any further. It must suffice to add very briefly, that he was a man of genius, and of sincere, ascetic piety. A collection of more than eight hundred letters, on all kinds of subjects, bear testimony to the diligence, justice, good sense, and kindness with which he administered the affairs of his See. He showed great political skill and firmness in his relations with the Lombards on one hand, and the Empire on the other. His ecclesiastical policy carried forward the pretensions of Rome towards that authority over the churches of Europe which it ultimately attained; he was an eloquent preacher; he made his mark on the services and music of the

Church; his writings, though he was not really a theologian of the first rank, were among the popular text-books of the early mediæval Church of Europe.

His "Morals" (*Magna Moralia*) were greatly admired, and his "Pastoral Care" (*Liber Pastoralis Curæ*) was translated into various languages. An Anglo-Saxon version was made by King Alfred, who sent a copy of it to every bishop in his kingdom, to be preserved in the cathedral church. It is the greatest of his writings, and is still a living work. In his *Dialogues* he gives incidentally his views of the condition of the soul after death, and puts forth the doctrine of a purgatory of purifying fire more distinctly than it had been stated by any previous writer.

We are always curious to know the personal appearance of the men whose lives have interested us, and his biographer, John the Deacon, gratifies this natural curiosity in the case of Gregory. He describes a picture which in his time existed in the hall of the Monastery of St. Andrew on the Cælian Hill, which contained the portraits of Gregory and his parents. The description of Gregory gives a minute analysis of every feature. He says that he was of just stature, but well formed:—Gregory of Tours, however, who paid a visit to his great namesake, has a good-natured remark, that it was remarkable that so great a man should be so small a person, which enables us to interpret John's complimentary epithet of "just" stature. John's statement that his face combined his father's length with his mother's roundness of visage is perhaps rather indefinite. He goes on to say that he had a large round tonsure, surrounded by dark hair curling under the ears, and with two little curls on the forehead turning towards the right; a yellowish (*sub-fulva*) beard of moderate dimensions; the eyes not large but well opened, and of hazel colour; the eyebrows long, slender, and arched; the nose slightly aquiline, thin where it descends from the eyebrows, broader about the middle, and expanded at the nostrils; the lips red, full, and well shaped; the chin rather prominent; the expression, as a rule, mild; with fine hands, taper fingers, and well-shaped nails. He is represented as habited in a chestnut-coloured planeta over a dalmatic, and a narrow pall adjusted round the shoulders in the manner shown by the mosaics of the period. He held the Gospels in the right hand and a cross in the left. A square nimbus behind the head indicated that he was still living, and that the picture was a portrait.

CHAPTER III

The Yorkshire Slave-Boys in the Roman Forum

When Gregory returned from Constantinople, he took up his position as abbot of his monastery, and the Pope Pelagius II. made him his secretary. Jerome held the same office under Damasus, and we gather from him that the duties were rather those of a secretary of state than of a mere scribe.

Bede records the tradition of the origin of the mission to Britain. Some merchants arrived in Rome, and on a certain day exposed many things for sale in the market-place, and abundance of people rushed thither to buy. Gregory went among the rest. His route would be by the road which runs through the valley between the Cælian and the Palatine Hills, past the Arch of Constantine, by the huge ruin of the Colosseum, and so into the Forum, the focus of the city's life, still surrounded by the ruins of the temples and palaces of its earlier splendour. Here was the market for all kinds of vendibles, and slaves were included among the chattels offered for sale. A group of these attracted the abbot's attention by the peculiarity of their appearance. In contrast with the brown skins and black hair and eyes of the native population, these were of large frame, with white bodies, beautiful faces, and hair of remarkable beauty. Having viewed them with interest, he asked from what country they were brought, and was told from the Island of Britain, whose inhabitants were of like personal appearance. He inquired whether the people of the island were Christians, or still involved in the errors of paganism, and was informed that they were pagans. "Alas! what a pity," he said, "that the author of darkness should be possessed of such fair countenances, and that while so beautiful in outward aspect their minds should be void of inward grace." He asked again, "What was the name of the nation to which they belonged?" and was answered that they were called Angles. "It is good," he said, "for they have angel faces, and it becomes such to be co-heirs with the angels in heaven." "And what is the name," he proceeded, "of the province from which they come?" He was told that the natives of the province were called Deira. "It is well," he said; "*De irâ*—withdrawn from the wrath of God, and called to the mercy of Christ." "And how is the king of the province called?" They told him his name was Ælle; and he answered, alluding to the resemblance of the name to Hallelujah, "It is fitting that the praise of God the Creator should be sung in those regions."[1]

The incident made a great impression upon the abbot's mind, and he conceived the idea of putting himself at the head of a band of missionaries and proceeding to the conversion of these interesting people.[2]

[1] John the Deacon, writing in the ninth century, tells the same story in nearly the same words.

[2] Gregory's biographers, John the Deacon and Paul the Deacon, differ as to the date of this incident; one says it was before Gregory went to Constantinople, and the other says after. It was probably in 586 or 587 A.D.

The bishop granted his request, and Gregory started with some companions. But when he was missed, and the cause of his absence was known, the people beset the Pope in St. Peter's and clamoured for his recall. He had already gone three days' journey when the messengers overtook him. The story runs that he was reading at midday while his companions rested, when a locust alighted upon his book. He called his companions' attention to it, and said, " *Locusta* signifies *Loco Sta*, Stay in this place, and portends that we shall not be allowed to continue our journey; but rise, saddle the beasts, and let us haste on our way as far as we are permitted." But while he spoke the messengers arrived to recall him, and he dutifully returned with them to the city.

Four or five years afterwards (590 A.D.), Gregory became Bishop. The early years of his pontificate were no doubt fully occupied with the pressing political dangers of the city and the manifold occupations of the See. But after six years (596 A.D.) the old design came again into his mind, and he began to look about for means of putting it into execution. A letter written in the early part of the year 596 seems to indicate one plan which occurred to him. He had recently sent one of his priests, Candidus, to take charge of a small estate at Marseilles belonging to the See of Rome. The oversight had usually been undertaken by the Bishop of Arles, on behalf of his brother of Rome, and the Bishop of Rome had paid his brother of Arles the compliment of sending him the pall in return for his services; but Gregory had come to suspect that the returns from the estate had not been so great as they ought to have been, so he sent an agent of his own to take charge of it. Gregory began about this time to adopt the same policy on the other distant estates of the See, because it gave him trustworthy agents of his own for the general business and interests of the See scattered in various countries. In the year 596 A.D., Gregory, in writing to Candidus, bids him, among other things, to look out for and purchase English and Saxon boys of seventeen or eighteen years of age, and send them to Rome; intending, no doubt, to have them educated and ordained and sent to preach to their fellow-countrymen.

It was a usual practice for wealthy people to have slaves carefully selected and educated for the higher duties of their households, for physician or secretary or steward, for tutor to the children, or man of letters, or singer or musician or artist. This is not the only example of slaves being trained up for the service of religion. Aidan of Northumberland used to buy the freedom of slaves, unjustly deprived of liberty, and educate them in his schools, and ordain some of them as priests. Before the end of the year, however, the bishop had adopted a speedier method and a larger plan.

Up to this time we know nothing of mission work undertaken by the Church of Rome, but we know that the conversions of the earlier centuries in the civilised countries of the world were undertaken on the apostolic model. St. Paul's work is that which is best known to us, and we remember that he was accustomed to take with him one or more companions, and to go from town to town, preaching. Many of the early missions were the solitary enterprise of a single enthusiast, as Patrick, Ninian, Birinus, Felix, in our own Church history. But the Celtic churches had adopted a different method. They were accustomed to send out a company of monks — the favourite number was an abbot and twelve monks, after the pattern of our Lord and His apostles—who should found a monastery in the country to be evangelized; to serve as a pattern of Christian life and a centre of Christian teaching. This method was largely adopted in subsequent times; and perhaps might be wisely used now in certain circumstances. For it seems as if the two methods were adapted to two different sets of circumstances; the one to the safety of travel and freedom of intercourse which existed in the Roman Empire, and to the work of presenting the new religion to the intelligence of civilised people; the other to the conditions of life among barbarous peoples.

Whether, in imitation of other missions, or from an independent view of its wisdom in the present circumstances, Gregory resolved to adopt the latter method, and to plant a Christian colony in the country which was the object of his solicitude. It was a bold and grand design, worthy of the great man who conceived it. He found the agents for its accomplishment ready to his hand in his own Monastery of St. Andrew's. He selected about thirty of its monks, and charged Augustine its prior with the leadership of the enterprise.

This is our earliest introduction to Augustine, the man who holds so distinguished a place in the history of the English Church. Of his parentage and previous life we know absolutely nothing. We shall have to study him for ourselves, as we are used to study a new acquaintance who suddenly enters into the sphere of our life to play an influential part in it, and slowly to form our opinion of him from his words and acts. There is this strong presumption in his favour at the outset, that the man whom Gregory chose as prior of his own convent, and then judged to be a fit man to take the lead in so important and difficult an enterprise, must have been a man of piety and ability, and a man to be trusted.

CHAPTER IV

THE DEPARTURE OF THE MISSION

IT might seem at first sight that it would require great preparations for the journey of so great a company for so long and difficult a journey. We are persuaded, on the contrary, that these monks set out, as all the groups of monks did who in subsequent times left the parent-house to found a new home, with nothing but each man his robe, staff, scrip, and water-bottle, and a pair of strong shoes. All the baggage they had besides, was half a dozen letters of introduction. These are addressed by Gregory to half a dozen Gallic bishops commending the travellers to their protection and assistance, viz., to Virgilius Arelatensis (of Arles), Pelagius Turnis (of Tours?), Protasius Aquæ Galliæ (of Aix-les-Bains), Desiderius Viennensis (of Vienne), and Syagrius Augustodunensis (of Autun). They carry also letters to Queen Brunhilda and her royal sons, Theodoric and Theodebert, and to Arigius the Patrician; thus securing for them the protection of the civil authorities of Gaul. The example of them which Bede has transcribed into his History, he says, was addressed to Ætherius, Bishop of Arles, in which he is mistaken, since it is certain, from the contemporary History of Gregory of Tours, that Virgilius was at that time Bishop of Arles. Ætherius was the name of the Bishop of Lyons, and it is very probable that

Gregory sent a copy of the letter to that bishop, as well as to his near neighbour of Vienne.

The letter is as follows:—

> "To the most Reverend and Holy Brother Ætherius, my Fellow-Bishop—Gregory, the Servant of the Servants of God.

"Although to priests who possess the charity which is pleasing to God, religious men need no one's recommendation, yet, since a suitable opportunity of writing offered itself, we have taken advantage of it to send this our letter to your Fraternity, to inform you that, for the welfare of souls, we have directed thither the bearers of these presents, Augustine, the servant of God, of whose earnestness we are assured, with other servants of God, whom it is requisite that your Holiness should hasten to help with friendly affection, and to give them your support. We have enjoined him to explain the business in detail, that you may the more readily give him your good aid, being sure that, when you are acquainted with it, you will, out of devotion to God, give all the help which the business requires. Moreover, we commend to your kindness in all things Candidus, the priest, our common son, whom we have sent to govern a small patrimony of our Church [[1] God keep you in safety, most reverend brother].—Given the tenth day before the Kalends of August [[1] in the fourteenth year of our most pious and august lord, Mauricius Tiberius, the thirteenth year after the consulship of our lord aforesaid], the fourteenth indiction," that is, the 23rd of July, in the year 596 A.D.

[1] These words are in the Letters of Gregory, but not in Bede's History.

In the Collection of the Letters of Gregory, we find this same letter addressed also to the Bishop of Marseilles and to the Bishop of Tours; another of the same general tenor, but differently worded, to Desiderius, Bishop of Vienne, to Syagrius of Autun, and to Protasius of Aix, and a separate letter to Virgilius of Arles. In the letter to Virgilius he adds a paragraph to the effect that his predecessor [probably not Licerius, but Sapandus], who had taken care of the little patrimony at Marseilles, had not accounted for some of the revenue due from it, and asking for restitution; and the letter to Protasius consists mainly of a request that he will urge Virgilius to make this restitution.

It is perhaps natural to suppose that the missioners would travel by the Aurelian Way, the great Roman road which skirted the Italian coast all round till it reached Provence, and then by Aix to Arles; then another Roman road, along the left bank of the Rhone, would take them northward to Vienne. We have to submit an alternative route for consideration.

First, let us look at these letters of introduction as a guide to the intended route. We observe that there are no letters to any place between Rome and Gaul. On the theory of the land journey, this could only be accounted for by supposing that there was nobody in the Lombard territory of North Italy, to whose good offices Gregory could commend his missioners. But this was not the fact. The Lombards, Barbarians and Arians as they were, had not destroyed the orthodox churches of North Italy, whose bishops would have shown all hospitality to those who came to them recommended by the great Roman Bishop. But it is true that the

Lombards were in possession of the country districts between the northern limits of the Roman Duchy, a few miles from Rome, and the city of Nice; and they were hostile to the Romans, continually committing outrages upon them, ravaging their fields up to the very gates of Rome, and carrying off their Roman captives into slavery. A company of Romans travelling across the country would therefore have been in great danger.

We submit that the monks avoided the toilsome journey and the perils of the way by a coasting voyage, which carried them without fatigue or danger from the Port of Rome to Marseilles, where they would find Candidus zealous in their service, and where their letters of introduction would ensure them influential countenance.

The conjecture, suggested by the probabilities of the case, is supported by several facts. First, by the fact that at a little later date, when Pope Stephen went to Gaul to appeal to King Pepin for aid, he avoided the whole Lombard country by taking the sea route; and secondly, by the fact that, at a still later period, Theodore, with Adrian and his monks, went by sea from Rome to Marseilles.[1]

If we wish to see with the mind's eye the start of an expedition of so much interest in our history, we must first picture the scene. The present Monastery of St. Andrew still occupies the same site on the north side of the Cælian Hill, conspicuous among the Seven Hills by its crown of pines, rising immediately behind the vast Colosseum, which the windows of the monastery overlooked; to the north of the Cælian rises the Palatine Hill, divided from it by the road which leads

[1] Bede, *Eccl. Hist.* iv. 1.

through the Arch of Constantine, and turns into the Forum. Upon this scene we may next place the actors in this memorable incident. We may picture the company of some thirty monks in their russet robes, equipped with staff and scrip, issuing from the great gate of the palatial monastery on the Cælian Hill, with the silver cross before them, and the picture of our Lord on a panel mounted as a banner, singing a litany; their brother monks on the terrace watching their departure, and the bishop at the gate with his hands raised in a parting benediction; a crowd of Romans, men, women, and children, with their flashing eyes and eager gestures, and loud *addios*, lining the sides of the hollow road as spectators; and we may accompany their procession along the twelve miles of dusty road to Ostia; and watch them embark on the good ship which the provident bishop has provided for their voyage, and wait on the seashore till the sails are lost to sight in the glow of the setting sun.

CHAPTER V

AT MARSEILLES

LANDING at Marseilles, Candidus would welcome them. The patrimony of St. Peter of which he was rector, was probably an estate in the neighbouring country, and its little house too small to entertain so large a company. But Candidus knows the city, and would easily arrange for their sojourn for a while to recover from the fatigues of their voyage, and to make their plans for the more difficult part of their journey. There were two monasteries in the city, they would be their appropriate resting-place, and both would be glad to offer hospitality to the monks of St. Andrew's, and to have the merit of assisting them in their glorious enterprise. Here, then, they would make some stay, Augustine probably visiting the neighbouring bishops to whom he had Gregory's letters of introduction, while his monks remained in their quarters. At Marseilles they would find merchants able to give them the best information about the journey which lay before them, and the prospect which awaited them at the end of it; for almost, a century before the Christian era, the agents of the commercial colony of Marseilles had visited the distant island in search of new markets, and during all the intervening time the intercourse between Britain and the Roman world which encircled the Mediterranean Sea had been carried on through the great Greek emporium.

They found Gaul full of trouble. It had long been in a state of intermittent civil war. In 561 A.D. the Frank territory was divided, according to the national custom, among the four grandsons of Clovis the Conqueror. Charibert held the Kingdom of Paris, Guntram of Orleans and Burgundy, Chilperic of Soissons, and Sigebert of Austrasia. These brothers were continually at war with one another. The chief interest gathers around Chilperic and Sigebert; the other two brothers played minor parts in the history; or rather, the interest centres in their queens, Fredegonda and Brunhilda, who were actuated by a deadly hate. The powerful Austrasian King was stimulated to action by Brunhilda, seeking vengeance for the wrongs of her sister, the former wife of Chilperic, who had been murdered by the agents of Fredegonda, with Chilperic's connivance—as it was believed, for the talented, versatile Chilperic was under the influence of the beautiful demon Fredegonda. Chilperic died, and was succeeded by his infant son, Chlotaire II., in whose name Fredegonda ruled over Neustria. In 593, three years before the point at which we have arrived in our history, Guntram had died, and Childebert succeeded to his dominions. In 596, Childebert died, and was succeeded by his two sons, Theodoric receiving Austrasia, and Theodebert the remainder of their father's dominions; they were both boys, and their able grandmother, Brunhilda, virtually ruled the greater part of the Frankish Empire in their names. Fredegonda died in the early part of 597 A.D., and there was peace for a few years, which might be at any moment, and soon actually was, broken by the ambitions of the rival sovereigns. It was during this pause in the chronic condition of civil war that Augustine and his party arrived. Still, since there was a cessation of hostilities, there was no immediate danger in the journey through France.

But the Italians had gathered still more unpleasant information of the condition of things in the country which was to be the scene of their future work. War still raged through the middle of the island from north to south, between the fierce heathen invaders and the civilised and Christian inhabitants of the land. In Northumbria, the precise goal of their journey, there were frequent wars between the rival royal houses of the two kingdoms of Deira and Bernicia into which it was divided, like the wars between the rival brother kings of France on a smaller scale; this was complicated with a war between the Northumbrians and the native Britons, who for many years after this time kept up a stubborn resistance, and even forty years afterwards (635 A.D.), under Cædwalla, actually reconquered the whole kingdom. Northumbria, at the best, was in the cold, bleak northern part of the land, and the Angles were a fierce and barbarous people; wars and rumours of wars everywhere. When brought face to face with it, the monks must have been greatly impressed with the universal disruption and confusion. It must have strengthened in their minds the general belief that the world was coming to an end. Accustomed as they were to the quiet of the cloister of their stately house in Rome, they were greatly alarmed at the prospect before them. Bede says: " They were seized with a sudden fear, and began to think of returning home rather than proceed to a barbarous, fierce, and unbelieving nation, to whose very language they were strangers." Augustine either shared their fears or was overpowered by their remonstrances, and consented to return to Rome and entreat Gregory that they might be relieved from " so dangerous, toilsome, and uncertain a journey." They did not know— how could they?—that out of the break-up of the old world a new and better world was rising up, and that they were to play no unimportant part in laying the foundations of the new order in one corner of that *ultima thule* of pagan barbarism, to lay the foundation-stone of that mighty fabric of a Christian England, destined to exercise so great an influence upon the future history of the world.

We may picture to ourselves, if we will, the moment when Augustine presented himself at the Palace of the Lateran; the grave, sorrowful amazement of Gregory; the head bowed with shame of Augustine, as he knelt at the feet of his abbot and bishop. We may imagine the gentle reproaches of Gregory, his unfaltering resolution, his spiritual encouragement; how he would point out that the dangers of the enterprise made it more glorious; that monks must not shrink from hardships; and that if death itself awaited them, death would be martyrdom; how he would express his grief that higher duties would not suffer him to go at once and put himself at the head of his faltering sons, and lead them in person to the holy war; and how he would gradually inspire his own lofty spirit into the heart of Augustine, and win from him the declaration to do or die.

Then would follow a sober consideration of practical measures. Augustine would report what he perhaps had in his mind when he consented to return to Rome; that the south-east portion of the island was more settled and civilised; that the king had lately married a Christian princess of the Franks, who had allowed a bishop to come in her train to minister to her; and that Kent would therefore offer a more favourable opening for their work than the wild Deira to which they had been sent. Gregory was a statesman and a man of good sense, and would recognise that this providential incident promised a safe footing for his mission to the English, and favourable circumstances for the beginning of its work. He sent Augustine back, strengthening his authority over his companions by giving him the formal position of their abbot; he also gave him some new letters, one to the monks themselves, another to Stephen the Abbot, and perhaps others. This is the letter to the monks:—

"Gregory, the Servant of the Servants of the Lord, to the Servants of our Lord.

"Since it were better not to begin a good work than to think of turning back from it when begun, it behoves you, most beloved sons, to accomplish the good work which, with the help of God, you have undertaken. Let not, therefore, the toil of the journey nor the tongues of men predicting evil deter you; but with all earnestness and zeal finish what, by God's direction, you have begun, knowing that a great labour is followed by a greater glory of eternal reward. When Augustine, your prior, whom I have now appointed to be your abbot, has returned to you, humbly obey him in all things, knowing that whatever you shall do by his direction will in all things be profitable to your souls. The Almighty protect you with all His grace, and grant me in the eternal country to see the fruit of your labour, so that, though I am unable to labour with you, I may be partaker with you in the joy of the reward, since I long, if it might be, to labour with you. God keep you in safety, most beloved sons.—Given on the tenth of the Kalends of August in the fourteenth year of our lord, Mauricius Tiberius, the most pious Augustus, in the thirteenth year after the consulship of the same our lord, in the fourteenth indiction (July 23, 596). [Same date as former letter to Virgilius of Arles.]

We may imagine how Augustine would enlarge upon the brief outline here laid down; how he would announce to his companions the change of their destination from bleak Northumbria and its fierce inhabitants to civilised, fertile Kent, where the protection of a Christian queen and the welcome of a Christian bishop awaited them; how he would impart to them the spirit of enthusiasm with which their great Bishop had rekindled his own zeal; how they would acknowledge his authority as their abbot, and promise to follow him to death, if such should be the will of God.

We are not so fortunate as to possess any description of the personal appearance of Augustine, such as John the Deacon has given us of his great master Gregory. His eleventh century eulogist, Gocelin, has given us, however, one striking trait by which we shall always be able in our mind's eye to distinguish

Augustine in the midst of his companions. He was of great stature, head and shoulders above the average of men. Few of his companions are known to us, even by name; among them were Peter, the first abbot of the monastery which Augustine founded at Canterbury, Laurentius who succeeded Augustine at his death as bishop, and Honorius who had been one of Gregory's youthful pupils, and was the precentor of the monkish choir; and Jacob the Deacon, who in after years accompanied Paulinus to Northumbria, may have been one of this original band.

CHAPTER VI

THE JOURNEY THROUGH FRANCE

THE Letters of Gregory belonging to this early period of the mission are grouped together and most of them without date. That to the monks, in reply to their request to be allowed to abandon the mission, is dated, X. Kal. Aug. of the fourteenth year of Maurice, the fourteenth indiction (July 23, 596 A.D.), and happily gives us an exact date for the setting out of Augustine from Rome the second time. That which is addressed to Pelagius of Tours and to Serenus of Marseilles is dated X. Kal. Aug. Indiction 14, with the year of the Emperor omitted, and was probably written at the same time. The letter to Abbot Stephen bears internal evidence that Augustine brought it back with him on his return from Rome, and is of some interest. In it Gregory thanks Abbot Stephen for his kindness to Augustine, and for a present of spoons and bowls, no doubt wooden spoons and bowls, the manufacture of the monks in their leisure time, which he had by Augustine sent as a present to the poor of Rome. One MS. allocates Stephen to Lerins, the little island off the coast of Nice where was a monastery which had a great reputation as one of the religious centres of the period. We gather, therefore, that Augustine visited this monastery from Marseilles after he had resolved to return to Rome. These two letters suggest that perhaps others of the group were given to Augustine at his second departure, but there is nothing by which we can discriminate them; and it is not of much importance, since all the letters are mere letters of introduction commending "the bearers of these presents, Augustine, the servant of God, whose zeal and piety are well known to us, and the other servants of God with him," to the good offices of the person addressed, and referring to Augustine himself for further information; they all also commend "Candidus, a priest, to whom we have committed the care of a small patrimony of our Church." The fact that Candidus, the Rector of the Patrimony at Marseilles, is mentioned in all the letters to be delivered along the route, seems to imply that Gregory had directed him to accompany the party and give them the advantage of his local knowledge of Gaul and its affairs. Some of the letters, however, demand a note.

In the letter to the Kings Theodoric and Theodebert, and that to their grandmother, the Regent Queen Brunhilda, Gregory addresses them by the title of Your Excellency; he pays them the rather far-fetched compliment of speaking of the Angles as their subjects; he announces as a reason for his mission that it has come to his knowledge that the nation of the Angles greatly desire to become Christian, but that the neighbouring bishops have no pastoral solicitude for them, and neglect them; therefore he has sent Augustine and others to go thither; also, he says he has directed Augustine to take with him some priests of the neighbourhood. What he means by saying that the Angles greatly desired to become

Christians it is difficult to understand; there is no known fact which justifies the statement except that the King of Kent had sought a Christian wife among the Franks. The neighbouring bishops, with whose want of pastoral zeal he finds fault, are of course the British bishops; Bede elaborates the same charge against them; there will be a better opportunity, in the sequel of the history, for considering the truth of the accusation. The priests of the neighbourhood whom Augustine is to take with him are probably Frank priests, to act as interpreters.

The importance of securing the permission and protection of the rulers of Gaul for the company of Italians passing through their territory is shown in the fact that a century later, when Archbishop Theodore and Abbot Hadrian passed through on their way to England, the abbot was stopped and detained for some time by Ebroin, the mayor of the palace, on the suspicion that he was a political emissary of the Eastern Emperor.

Augustine's mission party would, however, be tolerably sure of a good reception at court. However fierce and unscrupulous Queen Brunhilda may have been in pursuit of revenge against her enemy Fredegonda, she was a zealous supporter of religion; she had before this been in friendly communication with the great Bishop of Rome, and would willingly forward his wishes; besides, she would have a personal interest in the enterprise. Bertha, daughter of Charibert, who had gone to Kent as the wife of its King, was her niece, and Brunhilda would therefore take a natural interest in the missionaries who were going to the court of Kent, partly trusting to the influence of

Bertha for a good reception, and for the purpose of converting the Kentish men to the faith.

Then comes the letter to the Patrician Arigius. The title of Patrician, with which Eastern Emperors had graced the Barbarian Kings, whom they desired to conciliate, had by this time come down to their great officials. At this time Duke and Patrician seem to have been different titles of the same office, viz. that of commander of the armies and administrator of the royal affairs in a large territory; the latter title seems to be especially in use in the Burgundian kingdom. Arigius the Patrician was already in friendly relations with Gregory. For some years previously, when a vacancy occurred in the agency of the patrimony, Arigius, at Gregory's request, had received its income, and looked after its interests. This indicates that Arigius must have been stationed not far from Marseilles. Very probably he was the Frank official in authority in the south of France, and stationed perhaps at Arles, the chief city.

Just as the group of letters to the Bishops of Marseilles, Arles, and Aix indicate some stay in the south of France, so the two letters to the Bishops of Vienne and Lyons indicate the route of the travellers through Gaul. There was a Roman road along the left bank of the Rhone; but we think it most likely that our travellers saved themselves the toilsome march in the heat of summer by taking boat up the river; and we resume the journey with them.

At Vienne, the Roman character of the city would make them almost fancy themselves still in Italy; a portion of the portico of the ancient Forum still exists; and a temple supposed to have been dedicated to

THE JOURNEY THROUGH FRANCE 37

Augustus, and the remains of the theatre on the hillside, still remain. Here Augustine would present his letter of introduction to the Bishop Desiderius, and would hardly fail to be reminded that the Church of Vienne was the beginning of the Christianity of Gaul, when Pothinus and Irenæus came from the neighbourhood of Ephesus and planted the Church there. But it seems likely that the travellers would make no long stay here, since the great commercial emporium of the centre of France, Lyons, to which their ship would naturally be chartered, was only a few miles further up the river, and there they would have to halt and make arrangements for their further journey.

At Lyons they would therefore make some stay, and their letter to Bishop Ætherius would secure for them hospitality and assistance in their further arrangements. They would still, we think, prefer the convenience of water carriage; and another voyage of about one hundred miles up the Saône would bring them to Chalons, the usual residence of Queen Brunhilda and her royal grandson, Theodoric. Here again, therefore, they would halt and present their letters of introduction, and meet with a friendly reception, for, as we have seen, the able Queen was in friendly correspondence with the Bishop of Rome.

The next letter of introduction is addressed to Autun, which indicates that from Chalons the travellers would take a new departure, and would strike off north-westward. Here, therefore, the real hardships of the journey would begin, for water carriage would no longer be available, and weary marches for many days lay between them and the northern coasts of Gaul. At Autun they would halt and deliver their introduction to Syagrius, its bishop.

Autun had been a strong fortress and a great city from the early times of the Roman occupation of Gaul; the Roman gates, through which our travellers would pass, are fine works, and in very perfect preservation; and portions of the Roman wall and ruins of Roman buildings still remain to bear witness to its former greatness. Bishop Syagrius was a great man, a favourite of the all-powerful Queen, in correspondence with Gregory, and under recent obligations to him for the gift of the pall. Here, then, they would be certain of a welcome, and of all the aid of which they might be in need.

Two letters of introduction remain unaccounted for, first, that to Pelagius, Bishop of "Turnis." It is an unusual way of spelling Turonensis, but there was no other Gallic See of similar name, and Pelagius was Bishop of Tours at that time; he succeeded Gregory, the famous historian of Gaul, in the previous year; so that we cannot doubt that the letter is to the new Bishop of Tours. But that city was hundreds of miles to the westward of the route which Augustine must have taken.

The remaining letter is to Arigius, Bishop of Vapincum, *i.e.* Gap. But Gap was a little town, 2500 feet above the sea-level, among the Alps, a couple of hundred miles to the east of their route. Arigius was a very saintly person, and a great friend of Gregory, whom he had visited in Rome; the letter may have been intended to be forwarded by messenger, by way of friendly greeting, and to inform Arigius of the interesting work in hand.

The evidence of the route of our travellers, afforded by the letters of introduction, fails us at Autun; the probability is that thence they would make the best of their way northward along the well-frequented highroad to Gessoriacum (Boulogne), the usual port of embarkation for Britain, from before the days of Julius Cæsar down to the present day. At Gessoriacum they would probably halt for a few days to recover from the fatigue of their long march; and daily, from the hill on which the old town stood, would gaze wistfully across the channel to the opposite white cliffs of the island, the goal of their long journey. One fine morning, having taken farewell of Candidus, but taking with them the Frank interpreters, they would embark with a fair wind and set sail. Richborough would be the port for which they would make. It was the usual port of entry from the opposite shore, for Portus Lemanis (Lymne) could only be approached by a winding and difficult creek through the marshes; Dubriæ (Dover) was, and still is, in spite of modern improvements, dangerous in rough weather; Sandwich Bay, in those days—the passage is silted up now—afforded a safe entrance into the Wansum estuary, where the run of the tides formed the only drawback —for it was hardly a danger to those who knew their ways. Our voyagers would therefore make for the cliffs, and then coast along them north-eastward towards the gap in the white wall—from Walmer to Ramsgate—enter the estuary of the Wansum, and cast anchor in the narrow strait.

The wide tract of level land between Walmer and Ramsgate has undergone considerable changes in the intervening centuries between then and now. Then it was in great part covered with water. The little stream of the Stour, which now runs through the meadows and forms the boundary of the Isle of Thanet, was then an arm of the sea a mile wide, and made Thanet really an island, and ships bound up the Thames for the commercial emporium of London sailed through it, instead of passing as they must now do round the Foreland, and encounter the dangers of the sandbanks which beset the mouth of the Thames.

There were two harbours in the estuary of the Wansum—Rutupiæ, by that time known by the Saxon name of Richborough, was the principal port on the mainland of Kent. The old Roman fortress, situated upon a promontory above the level of the marshes, still stands, in places thirty feet high, with its square and round flanking towers, a relic of the Roman rule. But the little harbour of Ebbe's Fleet, on the opposite side of the estuary, was the port of the island; and it was there that Augustine and his company first set foot upon the land which was to be the scene of their future life and labours.

The authority for saying that Augustine landed at Ebbe's Fleet is Thorn, the fourteenth century monk of St. Augustine's; but there is other evidence that it was the usual landing-place for Thanet at an early date. Hengist and Horsa, St. Mildred, and the Danes, are all said to have landed there. Ebbe's Fleet is still the name of a farmhouse standing on a strip of high ground, rising out of the Minster Marshes, marked at a distance by the row of trees which crowns it; and, on a nearer approach, it is seen that it must once have been a headland or promontory running out into the sea between the two inlets of the estuary of the Stour on one side, and Pegwell Bay on the other. In early days a rock was shown here, on which it was said that Augustine placed his foot as he landed, and the impress of his foot remained on it as if it had been plastic clay. In later times it was said that St. Mildred landed there, and that it was her foot which left its miraculous mark, and a chapel dedicated to St. Mildred was erected over it.

CHAPTER VII

England in 596 a.d.

The fears which had beset them at Marseilles, and made them seek to turn back from their enterprise, would be allayed when they found themselves among civilised people, who treated them with consideration, and only required that they should wait till the will of King Ethelbert could be ascertained as to their further movements. Augustine sent a messenger to the King from Thanet, and waited for the answer, and for some days the party halted there; the Kentishmen, not unaccustomed to the sight of foreign visitors, yet wondering at this large company of Italians with their tonsured heads and strange monastic robes; the Italians eagerly studying the large, fair-complexioned, blue-eyed natives, among whom they were henceforth to live, and their strange, rude ways; each asking the other all kinds of questions through their Frank interpreters.

Here we may conveniently take our stand, and from this corner of the land consider the condition of the island and its people, as it would be presented to the Italians in answer to their inquiries.

Kent was the first part of the island which had been conquered by the Teutonic invaders. It is probable that its conquest had been effected with less violence, less disturbance of the native population, and therefore with less interruption of its prosperity, than some other parts.

The Jutes had come into the island one hundred and fifty years before (*c.* 450), and the grant of Thanet as the payment of their military services was the beginning of their kingdom. Oisc, the son of the mythic Hengist, was the first to take the title of King of Kent, and his descendants were called Oiscings; Oisc was the father of Octa, and he of Irminric, and he of Ethelbert, now reigning. The kingdom of the South Saxons had been founded to the west of them, and the kingdom of the West Saxons still further westward, and so the whole south of the country had been conquered and settled as far as the Avon on the borders of Wilts and Dorset by the year 516; soon afterwards the East Saxons had founded a kingdom in the country north of the Thames, and the East Angles in the eastern peninsula still to the north of Essex; and thus, by the year 577, the whole eastern side of the country, as far north as the Humber, had been conquered and settled.

The settlement of the respective territories and mutual relations of the independent bands of conquerors had not been effected without some appeals to the arbitrament of arms. When their boundaries had been adjusted, there was still a question of supremacy of one over the rest to be determined. Bede records that the first who exercised this supremacy "over all the southern provinces that are divided from the northern by the river Humber, and the borders contiguous to the same," was Ælle, King of the South Saxons, then it came to Ceawlin, King of the West Saxons, and then Ethelbert of Kent obtained it.

The subject of this dignity of Bretwalda,[1] which seems to mean Lord of Britain, is an obscure and difficult one. The probable explanation of it is, that when the imperial power was withdrawn from the province of Britain, the native people kept up the existing form of government as well as they could. This consisted in outline of a Vicar of Britain, in whom the civil administration centred, while the military command was divided between three officials; the Count of Britain had the general and supreme control; to the Count of the Saxon shore was committed the command of the troops and fortresses devoted to the defence of the eastern and southern shores; the Duke of Britain had the command of the troops and fortresses which protected the north and north-west. One and another of the Teutonic conquerors, it is conjectured, on defeating one of these native officials, assumed his title to himself, and, on being defeated in the contests which the conquerors waged among themselves, yielded it to the victor. We seem to see this very clearly in the case of Edwin of Northumbria, who, after his victory over Cadwallon, assumed the dignity of Bretwalda. His authority is spoken of (hyperbolically, no doubt) as extending throughout the island from sea to sea, and " his dignity was so great throughout his dominions that his banners were not only borne before him in battle, but even in time of peace, when he rode about his cities, towns, or provinces with his officers, the standard-bearer was wont to go before him. Also, when he walked along the streets, that sort of banner which the

[1] Bretwalda, Bretenanwealda, and Brytanwealda, are the three forms in which the title appears in the Saxon Chronicle.

Romans call *Tufa*,¹ and the English Tuuf, was in like manner borne before him." We should conclude, therefore, that Ælle, King of the South Saxons, had defeated the Count of the Saxon shore, and assumed his title as implying the rule of the conquered Roman British population, that he or his successor had been defeated by Ceawlin of the West Saxons, and had yielded the title as one of the spoils of victory, and that Ceawlin or his successor had in turn been defeated and had yielded the title to Ethelbert of Kent. We shall see in the sequel of the story that the title implied a real and effective authority over the subject kings.

King Ethelbert, thus, as we have said, was a powerful King, ruling his own Kentishmen in peace and prosperity, and exercising supremacy over the whole south-east of the island, northward to the Humber, and westward to the Dorset Avon. But this was the whole of the island which was at this time peacefully subject to the Teutonic conquerors. Beyond these limits the slow war of the two races still raged.

The Angles of Northumbria were still engaged in chronic hostilities with the Britons of Strathclyde, and the final issue was still doubtful. Bands of adventurers were gradually winning for themselves settlements in the middle of the country, destined to coalesce into a kingdom of Mercia, but another thirty years had to elapse before Mercia had spread over middle England, and sixty years before the Briton ceased to dispute the possession. On the Welsh border the war still raged, and conquest did not reach its limit for nearly two centuries. On the border of

---

¹ A globe or a tuft of feathers fixed on a spear.

West Wales (Dorset, Devon, and Cornwall), also the same chronic strife existed, and the stubborn defence of the native Romanised population was only slowly driven back. In summarising our national history, the fact is often imperfectly recognised, in the long perspective of time, that the Anglo-Saxon conquest lasted over about two hundred years, and that no part of the Roman Empire made so stubborn and prolonged a resistance to the Barbarian conquest as the ex-province of Britain. Indeed, the natives of the Cornish peninsula did not lose their independence till the reign of Athelstane, in the tenth century; Wales did not finally submit to the conqueror till the fourteenth century, and we are the witnesses of a recrudescence of the national spirit in the contemporary demand for Welsh Home Rule.

We have already had occasion to notice that Ethelbert had sought to ally himself in marriage with the house of Clovis, and that Bertha, the daughter of Charibert, had been given to him, on condition that she should retain the free exercise of her religion, and that Liudhard, Bishop (of Senlis?), had accompanied her to Kent. The Queen would probably have some Frank female attendants, and the bishop would very likely be accompanied by a deacon at least, so that there was a little group of Christians already at the Kentish court. Their personal influence ensured a friendly reception to the Italian visitors; but even without it, Ethelbert was sufficiently civilised, and sufficiently in touch with the social and political life of the Continent, to have offered no violence to a company of peaceful men sent by the illustrious Bishop of Rome, and with the good wishes of the Frank kings.

Accordingly, the messengers to the King sent by the man in authority at Ebbe's Fleet, to know what was to be done about these bands of Italian strangers, brought back a peaceful reply; they were to remain for the present where they were, and to be supplied with all which was necessary, until the King should come and hear what they had to say.

After a short delay, Ethelbert came to the island and gave Augustine and his companions audience. The King arranged that the interview should take place in the open air, from a superstitious belief that any magical influence which the strangers might possess would be less effectual in the open air than in a house. It is the unaccustomed which creates fear. The imagination of the dweller in cities peoples the weird heath and the silent forest with shapes of fear; the dweller in the open country fears the cramping labyrinth of the streets, and the darksome nooks and corners of houses built by men. A very ancient oak, on a rising ground about the middle of the Isle of Thanet, was for centuries believed to be the very tree under whose spreading boughs the momentous interview was held; an obelisk now marks the spot. We may picture the Kentish King seated on his chair beneath the oak, and Queen Bertha would not be absent on an occasion of so great interest to her; about the King, his counsellors and armed attendants; about the Queen, her bishop-chaplain, and her female attendants; and a crowd of Kentish people—men, women, and children—as spectators. The strangers came upon the ground in a way which must have made a strong impression upon the imagination of the beholders. When we pictured them as leaving their monastery at Rome, it was a picture reflected back from this occasion, on which we are expressly told that they came to the interview in procession. A tall silver cross preceded them; the picture of the Saviour —the solemn Byzantine type of face which we still see in the ancient mosaics—was carried like a banner in the midst; the forty monks, in their russet robes and cowls, walked with slow step, two and two; Honorius, the youthful chorister, first, and the tall form of Augustine closing the procession; and as they approached they sang a litany, in which they prayed for the salvation of those to whom they had come.

Augustine sat down at the King's command, and, through the medium of the Frank interpreters, preached to the listening people the Word of Life. The King's reply was not wanting in dignity and good sense : " Your words and promises," he said, " are plausible, but since they are new and doubtful, I cannot at once assent to them, and leave the customs which I have so long observed with the whole English race. But since you have come hither, strangers from a great distance, and I see clearly that what you yourselves believe to be good and true, you wish to impart to us, we do not wish to molest you; nay rather, we are anxious to receive you hospitably, and to give you all that is needed for your support, nor do we hinder you from doing all you can to win people to the faith of your religion." If the words of the King were full of encouragement, his actions more than fulfilled the promise of his words, for he directed the strangers to go to his capital, and made arrangements there for their lodging and maintenance.

They would be ferried across the strait to Richborough, and accomplish the last stage of their long journey on foot, along the Roman road. At length, from the summit of St. Martin's Hill, they would come in sight of their future home; a city in the meadow, beside the little river Swale, surrounded by Roman walls, with some Roman buildings of mixed brick and stone, standing lofty and massive among the low timber houses of the English. A little to the left, outside the city, they would see the recently repaired Roman Church of St. Martin, in which Bishop Liudhard maintained the divine service for Queen Bertha and her people. Here they again formed themselves into procession, and entered the city amidst the wonder of the townspeople, singing: "We beseech Thee, O Lord, in all Thy mercy, that Thy anger and wrath be turned away from this city, and from Thy holy house, because we have sinned. Hallelujah!"

CHAPTER VIII

THE RECEPTION OF THE MISSION

THE boundaries of the Kingdom of Kent were the same as those of the modern county, but the condition of the country was very different. The extensive forest of Andred covered a great part of the south-west of the country, dense woods fringed the borders of Romney Marsh, another great tract of woodland spread beyond Canterbury to the north. The Weald of Kent, a ridge of hills covered with scrub, extended through the middle of the country.

Only a small portion of the land was occupied, and it is hard to realise how small was the population.[1] The Roman fortresses, by which the coast had been protected from the Saxon pirates, Rutupiæ (Richborough), Dubræ (Dover), and Portus Lemanis (Lymne), must have been in good preservation then, and possibly garrisoned; the other Roman towns of Regulbium (Reculver), Durovernum (Canterbury), and Durobrivæ (Rochester), seem to have survived storm and sack, and perhaps still existed partly in ruins, but more or less inhabited. Roman roads ran from Richborough, through Canterbury and Rochester, to London; others from Canterbury to Dover and to Lymne, and from

[1] The population of all England four centuries later was only two millions.

Richborough to Dover; and still another branched off from the main London road to a spot opposite the Roman town at East Tilbury, on the north side of the Thames, where a ferry across the river formed the usual passage between the two countries of Kent and Essex.

There is a question of considerable importance in the history of this period, which is still under discussion and awaiting further archæological discoveries for its determination : to what extent the Romano-British population was slaughtered by, or driven away before, the Teutonic conquerors. The general course of the conquest of Italy by the Goths, and of Gaul by the Franks and Burgundians, was that, on the defeat of the Roman armies, the country submitted to its new masters. The cities capitulated, and were allowed to retain their old municipal life under their own magistrates and laws; the Barbarian king requiring nothing more than the tribute and service which had been rendered to the Emperor. Land was demanded for the new settlers, but with remarkable consideration for old proprietors.

The Barbarian tribes who fell upon Britain were more fierce and barbarous than the Goths and Franks, who had long been in contact with the Empire, while Britain was disorganised and less able to hold its own against the invaders. It has been held by some historians, that the Jutes, Saxons, and Angles waged a war of extermination, storming and sacking every town and massacring the inhabitants, and slaying all the inhabitants of the open country who failed to make their escape. The very neighbourhood at which we have arrived affords an actual example of the destruction of a town, for the history expressly says that Anderida, a town on the Sussex side of the great forest which covered half Kent, was stormed and not a soul left alive in it. On the other hand, it is maintained by others that such ruthless warfare was contrary to the habits of the Teutonic people, that there are many evidences that the life of some of the towns continued through the crisis, and that many of the native inhabitants of the open country retained their places on the soil, and submitted to and were spared by the conquerors.

Without entering into the general question, we venture to say that there are reasons for thinking that in Kent at least some of the towns survived the conquest, or at least were speedily rebuilt and re-peopled, and that many of the Britons remained in the country places. To begin with, the Jutes obtained their first footing in the Isle of Thanet by its cession to them; and they were for some time in friendly relations with the neighbouring people. Their mastery over the rest of Kent seems to have been determined by the result of several great battles, two of which, the history tells us, were fought at Crayford, and the defeated Britons fled towards Londinium. This looks like the effort, not of the natives of Kent to defend their own land, but like an effort on the part of the British authorities—it was the beginning of the conquest, and the British organisation was not yet broken up—to defeat and expel the invaders. The native inhabitants would find near and inaccessible places of refuge from a force which they could not resist, in the woods, the weald, the forest, and the marshes. The towns were all in positions in which the advantages of situation, and the necessities of society, required that towns should be; at the ports—Regulbium, Rutupiæ, Dubræ, and Lemanis; along the great roads—at Durovernum, Durolevum, and Durobrivæ, through which the intercourse of the country with the Continent passed. The conquerors, after all, were few in number, and could not profitably occupy the whole of the cultivated land; and it seems likely that, while seizing all they wanted, they would leave the conquered people to live upon the remainder.

But one thing seems certain, that the heathen conquerors had stamped out the Christian religion.

We are specially concerned at present with the city of Durovernum, to which the new inhabitants had given the new name of Cantwara-byrig, into which we have seen the Italian mission enter in procession, with cross and banner and chanted litany. Externally its walls and gates gave it the aspect of a Roman city, and our band of monks might be encouraged by the thought that they were entering a city like one of those of Gaul, through which they had lately passed in their long pilgrimage. Internally they would find a different state of things. It was the capital of the Jute Kingdom, which had been in a condition of settled prosperity for one hundred and fifty years. The houses of the Roman towns in Britain had usually only foundations of masonry and walls of timber; a storm and sack and conflagration, if that had been the fate of Durovernum, would leave a heap of ruins. But the charred timbers and heaps of roof-tiles would have been long since cleared away, and new houses built by the Jute inhabitants, and there must have been by this time a new town built within the old walls, full of the life which belonged to what is expressly called by Bede "the capital of all the dominions" and the seat of the court of Ethelbert, King of Kent, and Bretwalda. The fact that the King looked beyond the families of the kings of the East or South Saxons or the East Angles, and sought a bride from the great house of Clovis, throws some light upon the situation. It indicates that he was a powerful and prosperous king, who might fairly aspire to so distinguished a matrimonial alliance; that he had relations with France and with the Frank kings; that the relatives of Bertha were willing to compromise the religious question shows that they recognised that the alliance was not beneath their dignity; and, notwithstanding this difficulty, the daughter of Charibert, the grandson of Clovis, was content to marry Ethelbert of Kent.

Canterbury, then, would be a thriving Teutonic town within its old Roman walls. There would be some of the buildings of the Roman period still standing, for Roman brick and mortar are almost indestructible. There would be remains, at least, of temple and courthouse and theatre. But what concerned Augustine, and concerns us, is that among the old Roman buildings of the city there was a church, disused and in disrepair, for it had been empty for a century, but with its walls at least still standing in all the solidity of Roman construction. The temporary dwelling-place which Ethelbert assigned them is said to have been in Stable Gate[1] or Staple Gate, in the extreme north part of the city, now the North Gate, by which they entered into it.

[1] Thorn.

Bede says that as soon as they entered it "they began to imitate the course of life practised in the primitive Church; applying themselves to frequent prayer, watching, and fasting; despising all worldly things as not belonging to them; preaching the Word of Life to as many as they could, receiving only their necessary food from those they taught; living themselves in all respects conformably to what they prescribed to others; and being always disposed to suffer any adversity, and even to die, for that truth which they preached."

The passage is a litle rhetorical, and the last clause of it inevitably provokes the remark that there was not much danger now of adversity or death, and that when there was, at the beginning of their journey, they were anxious to turn back. But we may take it as an assurance that they at once resumed the monastic course of life interrupted by their long journeying, with its numerous day and night services of prayer, and its ascetic observances, and began with zeal their work of evangelisation. There is perhaps nothing more striking, in its way, to a people who have no experience beyond the average life of worldly occupations and aims, than such a sight as that which this Italian community presented to the honest, simple, worldly-minded Teutons around them. It is very possible, we repeat, that if some of our modern missions were commenced in a similar way—*mutatis mutandis*—they might have greater success. In this case at least it was successful. "Some, admiring the simplicity of their innocent life and the sweetness of their heavenly doctrine, believed and were baptized."

At first, " till the King, being converted to the faith, allowed them to preach openly and build or repair churches in all places," they used the Church of St. Martin, just without the walls, for their more public services—for mass and preaching and baptizing; and we suppose that at this time the work of the missionaries was limited to the maintenance of their own religious life in their own habitation, and to public ministrations in the privileged Queen's chapel.

Some relics of this venerable church still remain; for though the present Church of St. Martin at Canterbury is a building of much more recent date, many Roman bricks, easily recognised by their dimensions and texture, are used in the building, and are in all probability part of the material of the original Roman-British church on the same site.

CHAPTER IX

The Success of the Work

We come now to a series of interesting events, which it is important, but difficult, to arrange in chronological order. The events are the conversion and baptism of Ethelbert, the consecration of Augustine, a grand baptism of ten thousand converts one Christmastide, and a letter from Gregory to Queen Bertha. Bede says, in the 26th chapter of the First Book of the *Ecclesiastical History*, which is our main authority for the whole story, that after the King was baptized, greater numbers began daily to flock together to hear the Word, and were united to the Church. Then, at the beginning of the next chapter, he says: "In the meantime Augustine was consecrated, and sent Laurentius the Priest and Peter the Monk to Rome to acquaint Gregory that the nation of the English had received the faith, and that he was himself made their bishop."

Bede says nothing of the baptism of the ten thousand, and does not give the letter to Bertha; we get these incidents from the Letters of St. Gregory. Now, these letters are for the most part undated; they have been arranged by learned editors, who have bestowed much learning and ingenuity upon the task, in a chronological order which is probably approximately right in the great majority of cases, but which is open to challenge in the case of any undated letter. In one of these undated letters, which the editors assign to June, 598 A.D., addressed to Eulogius, Bishop of Alexandria, Gregory tells him the glad tidings that a monk of his, whom he had sent with some companions to the nation of the English, and had caused to be made a bishop, had had so great a success that he had on the previous Christmas baptized ten thousand souls.

Gregory's letter to Queen Bertha is placed by the editors among a batch of letters which were sent by Gregory to England in the year 601. Some of these letters are dated, others are not; one which is dated is addressed to Ethelbert, and shows that Ethelbert was at that time a Christian. This, which is not dated, is addressed to Queen Bertha, and implies that Ethelbert was not a Christian, for it blames his wife for it, and exhorts her to use her influence for his conversion.

The difficulty arises in this way, that Bede does not give us dates for the baptism of Ethelbert and the consecration of Augustine; and though he mentions them in this order, yet the "meanwhile" with which he introduces the last-mentioned event leaves it doubtful whereabout in the preceding narrative it is to be introduced, whether before or after the first-mentioned event. The later biographers of Augustine —Gocelin, 1098 A.D.; Thorn, 1397 A.D.; and Elmham, 1412 A.D.—were monks of St. Augustine's monastery, and give the tradition of the monastery; and they say that Ethelbert was baptized on Whitsunday 597 A.D., and Gregory was consecrated on November

THE SUCCESS OF THE WORK

16th of the same year; but the tradition is too late to be of much authority without confirmatory evidence, and cannot stand against any contemporary contradictory evidence. On a review of the whole case, we shall take leave to assume that the order of events is—the consecration of Augustine, the baptism of the ten thousand, the letter to Bertha, and lastly the conversion of Ethelbert; and on the last two points we shall have more to say when they occur in the narrative.

Soon after Augustine's return thither from Rome, which he left 23rd July, 596 A.D., the Italian mission started from Southern Gaul. They would be anxious to reach their destination, there was no reason for delay, and it was a good season of the year for travelling. Even if they made the whole journey on foot, three months would be sufficient time for its accomplishment. We conclude, therefore, that they arrived in the course of the autumn. With very little further delay they were settled in temporary quarters in Canterbury, resumed their monastic life, and commenced their mission work.

The tradition of St. Augustine's monastery was that Augustine was consecrated, 16th November 597. We have already learned from Bede, in general terms, that the work was successful; we suppose that by the autumn of the following year Augustine felt that, with the King friendly and inclining towards Christianity, though not yet converted, with the support of the Queen, and with a considerable body of converts, he had secured a safe and permanent footing in the island, and that the time had come for establishing the Church among the English by seeking consecration for himself as its bishop. His next proceeding was clearly according to instructions given him by Gregory, though they are not anywhere recorded. He proceeded to Gaul to seek consecration as bishop of the new Church which he had founded among the English. He did not seek consecration from Liudhard on the spot, and he did not go to the nearest Gallic bishops, but retraced his steps across the whole breadth of Gaul to Arles, and there received the episcopal order at the hands of Virgilius. It is clear that Gregory had requested Virgilius, as Metropolitan of Gaul and Gregory's representative, to act in this matter. Indeed, in the letter to Eulogius of Alexandria, he says expressly that the Gallic bishops consecrated by his desire.

The monastic biographers gave 16th November 597 as the date of Augustine's consecration. He must have hastened back if he was present at the great baptism of the ten thousand, which is assigned by the editors of Gregory's Letters to Christmas of the same year. This great triumph of the faith, according to the mediæval tradition, did not take place at Canterbury, but in the river Irwell, somewhere about the place where it flows into the Medway, and therefore denotes the successful result of some special work by the missionaries in that neighbourhood.

Gregory's letter shows that it was not till after Christmas 597 A.D., it would probably not be till the spring of 598 A.D., that Augustine sent two of his best men—Laurence the Priest and Peter the Monk—to Rome, to give a full report of all that had happened. It was on the return of these messengers, we submit, that Gregory sent the letter to Queen Bertha (which has been placed by Gregory's editors among a batch sent in 601 A.D.), by the hands of Laurentius the Priest and Mellitus the Abbot.

It was part of the wise policy of Gregory to seek to exercise an influence over sovereigns through their wives.

It was still a characteristic of the Teutonic nations in those days, as it was in the earlier times of Tacitus, that their women were highly esteemed, and exercised a great social influence. We need not go beyond the limits of our own Church history to see that this esteem and influence were the result of their own virtues. In the history of royal and noble families of the English kingdoms of this period, a very remarkable feature is that so many of the women were not only comparatively educated, refined, and religious, but also of great force of character and strength of principle. It is enough to point, in illustration of it, to the considerable number of double monasteries, in which learning, art, civilisation, and religion flourished under the administration of royal and noble abbesses. Another remarkable feature of the history is the influence which queens actually exercised in the introduction of the Church into the English kingdoms—Bertha into Kent, Ethelburga into Northumbria, Elfleda into Mercia, and Ebba into Sussex. Gregory acted wisely, therefore, in corresponding with Brunhilda in France, and Theodelinda in Lombardy, and Constantia in Constantinople itself, and now with Bertha in England.

This is a suitable place for recording the little we know of Ethelbert's Frankish Queen. Her parents were Charibert, one of the four grandsons among whom the conquests of Clovis were divided, and Ingoberga, whose name indicates a Scandinavian parentage. Charibert was a man of intellectual ability and versatility beyond the average of his time. He valued the Roman civilisation of his Gallic subjects, and encouraged its extension to his Franks. He prided himself upon his mastery of the Latin language and his knowledge of Roman law, and his skill as a judge. He was less favourably distinguished for the Oriental licence which he assumed in the matter of wives and concubines. He reached a crisis in this respect when he took two sisters—Mariovefa and Merofleda—from among his wife's attendants as his concubines. Ingoberga tried to make him ashamed of his low tastes, by allowing him to find their father, a mechanic, engaged in some work of his trade about the palace. Instead of shame, the tacit rebuke only led to anger and defiance. Charibert deserted his Queen, and married Mariovefa. The Bishop of St. Germains excommunicated them both, but Charibert would not give up the unlawful connection. Ingoberga retired to Le Mans with her only daughter, Bertha, and there lived a life of religious seclusion. Charibert died not long after this, in 575 A.D., while Ingoberga survived by nearly a quarter of a century, dying in 594 A.D. The date of Bertha's marriage is not known. When Bede says that Ethelbert received her "*a parentibus*," we cannot safely infer that it was in the lifetime of her parents, because the phrase may mean from her relations. We must not always take the courtly compliments of Gregory too literally, they were the fashion of the time; but Bertha's education and training by her saintly mother in her religious seclusion at Le Mans may well have entitled her to the character which the great Bishop gives her in his letter—that she was established in the true faith, and well instructed in learning.

It will suffice to give the substance of Gregory's letter to the Queen. He tells her that Laurence the Priest and Peter the Monk, on their return from Britain to Rome, have informed him how great have been the kindness and assistance which she has bestowed upon his very reverend brother and fellow-bishop, Augustine, and that he has returned thanks to Almighty God, who has graciously condescended to reserve the conversion of the nation of the Angles as her reward. He goes on to tell her that, as through Helena of famous memory, the mother of the most pious Emperor Constantine, the hearts of the Romans had been kindled to the Christian faith, so he trusted that God's goodness would effect the same results through her care for the nation of the Angles. Then comes a sentence which proves that the letter is misplaced among those of 601 A.D., and induces us to transfer it pretty confidently to this place, since it seems to assume that Ethelbert was not yet a Christian, to blame his wife for it, and to urge her to undertake his conversion. "And indeed," he says, "long since, you ought to have inclined the mind of our glorious son, your husband, to seek the safety of his own soul and of the kingdom, to embrace the faith which you adore, so that there might be joy in heaven over his conversion and that of the whole nation, and reward to you"; and adds that, "seeing she was established in the true faith, and well endowed with learning, this ought not to be a long or difficult work; but since now by God's will the time is suitable, make up by increased exertion for the past neglect." The letter itself states that it was written after Laurence and Peter had arrived in Rome, who were sent by Augustine to acquaint Gregory "that the nation of the English had received the faith of Christ, and that he himself was made their bishop." The only way of explaining the matter seems to be that the letter to Bertha was sent back at once by Laurence and Peter in 597 A.D., not by Laurence and Mellitus in 601 A.D.; and that the announcement that "the nation of the English had received the faith of Christ" did not include the King, but, on the contrary, purposely omitted his name; and that the letter to Bertha has been assigned to the later date in error. Returning to the letter, Gregory goes on to urge the Queen: "Therefore, by constant persuasion strengthen the mind of your glorious husband in the love of the Christian faith, let your solicitude for him infuse increase of love to God, and so kindle his mind and the minds of those subject to him with the fullest conversion, that both he may offer a great sacrifice to Almighty God through the earnestness of your devotion, and that those things which are told of you may grow and be every way approved. For your good deeds have come to be known not only to us Romans, but to many places, and even to Constantinople and to the most serene Prince (viz. the Eastern Emperor); so that not only Christians rejoice, but there is joy among the angels in heaven." He concludes by commending the afore-mentioned, his very reverend brother and fellow-bishop and the servants of God, "whom we have sent with him for the conversion of your nation," and hopes that she may reign happily with her glorious husband, and after many years receive the joys of the future life which knows no end.

CHAPTER X

Gregory's Instructions

Gregory also sent back by Laurence and Peter a long letter to Augustine, in reply to questions which the quondam prior had submitted to his quondam abbot. It is not the only evidence that, so long as he lived, Gregory took an active interest in the affairs of the English mission, and that Augustine dutifully received the counsels and reproofs of his old master. Gregory's replies embody Augustine's questions; it will suffice to make some extracts from the Letters.

"1. Concerning bishops, how are they to behave themselves towards their clergy? Into how many portions are the things given by the faithful to the altar to be divided? and how is the bishop to act in the church?"

Gregory answers:—

"Holy Scripture, and especially St. Paul's Epistle to Timothy, answers the question. But it is the custom of the Apostolic See to prescribe this rule to all bishops, newly ordained, that all the stipend which accrues should be divided into four portions—one for the bishop and his family, for hospitality and maintenance, another to the clergy, a third to the poor, and the fourth for the repair of churches. But since your Fraternity was brought up under monastic rules, it does not become you to live apart from your clergy in the Church of the English, which, by God's help, has lately been brought to the faith; you are to follow that course of life which our fathers did in the infant Church, when none of them said that anything which he possessed was his own, but all things were in common to them."

[In Letters of Gregory there is inserted here another question: "I desire to know whether clerics who cannot be continent may marry, and if they marry, whether they ought to return to the world." To which there is the same answer which we find in Bede]:—

"If there are any clerics, not in holy orders, who cannot live continent, they should take wives and receive their stipends outside (the community), because we know it is written in the authorities above mentioned, that distribution was made to every man according to his need. Their stipends are therefore to be cared for and provided, and they are to be kept under ecclesiastical rules, that they may live orderly and attend to singing of Psalms, and, by the help of God, keep their hearts and tongues and bodies from all unlawful things. But for those living in common, why need we say anything about assigning portions, or maintaining hospitality, or fulfilling works of mercy, since everything beyond your needs is to be expended in pious and religious works, and since our Lord and Master says as to all which remains, 'Give alms of such things as ye have, and behold all things are clean to you' (Luke xi. 41)'?"

Augustine's second question:—" 2. Since the faith is one, why are the customs of the Churches different—

one use of the mass exists in the Roman Church, and another is observed in the Churches of Gaul?"

Answer of the blessed Pope Gregory:—

"Your Fraternity knows the use of the Roman Church, in which you remember you were brought up; but it seems good to me that if you have found anything in the Roman or Gallican, or any other Church, which may be more acceptable to Almighty God, you should carefully select it, and introduce into the Church of the English, which is still new in the faith, whatsoever you can gather from the several Churches. For things are not to be loved for the sake of places, but places for the sake of things. From them choose things which are pious, religious, and right, and, having collected them into one packet (*fasciculum*), place them in the minds of the English as their use.

Augustine's third question:—" 3. I pray you to inform me what he ought to suffer who shall take a thing from the Church by theft."

Answer of the blessed Pope Gregory:—

"It depends upon the person who has committed the theft; for some steal who are not in need, and some steal through want. Therefore some must be punished by fine, and some by stripes, some with greater severity, and some more mildly. And when greater severity is used, it is to proceed from charity, not from anger, for this is done to him who is corrected, lest he be delivered up to hell. . . . You may add that they ought to restore those things which they have stolen from the Church, but far be it from the Church to receive profit from those things which she seemed to lose, and seek gain out of her losses."

To the fourth question, whether two brothers may marry two sisters, Gregory answered, "There is nothing in Scripture which seems to forbid it."

Augustine's fifth question:—" 5. To what degree may the faithful marry their kindred, and whether it is lawful for men to marry their stepmothers and cousins?"

Answer of the blessed Pope Gregory:—

"A law of the Roman commonwealth permits cousins to marry, but we have found by experience that the offspring of such wedlock cannot thrive; and the divine law forbade a cousin to uncover the nakedness of his kindred (Lev. xviii. 6, 7); hence they must be of the third or fourth generation of the faithful who can lawfully join in matrimony. To marry one's mother-in-law is a heinous crime, because it is forbidden in the law. It is also prohibited to marry a sister-in-law, for the same reason.

"But since there are many of the English who, whilst still in unbelief, are said to have been joined in this wicked union, when they come to the faith they are to be admonished that they abstain, and be made to know that this is a grievous sin. Let them fear the dreadful judgment of God, lest, for the gratification of their carnal appetites, they incur the torments of eternal punishment. Yet they are not on this account to be deprived of the communion of the body and blood of Christ, lest we should seem to avenge upon them the things which any did through ignorance before they had received baptism. For at this time the holy Church chastises some things through zeal, and connives at and endures others through discretion, so that by this forbearance and connivance she may often suppress the evil which she disapproves. But all that come to the faith are to be admonished not to do such crimes, and if any shall be guilty of them, they are to be excluded from the communion of the Body and Blood of Christ. For as the offence is, in some measure, to be tolerated in those who do it through ignorance, so it is to be severely punished in those who do not fear to sin knowingly."

Augustine's sixth question:—" 6. Whether a bishop may be ordained without other bishops being present, in case there is so great a distance between them that they cannot easily assemble?"

Answer of the blessed Pope Gregory:—

" As for the Church of the English, in which you are as yet the only bishop,[1] you can no otherwise ordain a bishop but in the absence of other bishops. When bishops come over from Gaul, they may be present to you as witnesses in ordaining a bishop. But we wish your Fraternity so to ordain bishops in England that they shall be separated by as short an interval as possible, ... and when this shall be the case, then no bishop is to be ordained without the presence of three or four bishops...."

Augustine's seventh question:—" 7. How are we to deal with the bishops of France and Britain?"

Answer of the blessed Pope Gregory:—

" We give you no authority over the bishops of France, because the Bishop of Arles received the pall in ancient times from my predecessors, and we are not to deprive him of the authority which he has received. Augustine may point out faults, etc., to the Bishop of Arles, but not attempt to exercise jurisdiction.

[1] This seems to imply that Liudhard had returned to Gaul or was dead.

"But as for all the bishops of Britain we commit them to your care, that the unlearned may be taught, the weak strengthened by persuasion, and the perverse corrected by authority."

The eighth and ninth questions contain some matters with which it is not expedient to deal here; it may suffice to say that they imply that it was then the custom for women to come to church to return thanks after childbirth, and Gregory cites the Old Testament custom as to the time, but says that she sins not if she comes earlier; and that a child may be baptized the very hour it is born.

These questions and answers need a few observations. The rule of fourfold division of the Church's revenues, which Gregory says was that laid down by the Roman See, would no doubt be adopted by Augustine in the churches to which he gave law; but there is no evidence that this rule was adopted by the churches afterwards founded by the Celtic missionaries.

The "clerks, not in holy orders," would be those in minor orders, subdeacons, etc.

The difference between the Roman and Gallican Liturgies arose from the fact that they belonged to different families of the primitive liturgies, the one to that known as the Roman Liturgy, or the Liturgy of St. Peter, the other to that known as the Ephesine Liturgy, or the Liturgy of St. John. The breadth of view which dictated Gregory's direction to Augustine to select from every Church that which was best, and compile a Liturgy for the English, is characteristic of the man who himself revised the Roman Liturgy, and introduced new features into it. What Augustine did in the matter is not accurately known. He would find Liudhard using the Gallican Liturgy in St. Martin's, and if he made inquiry he would learn that the British Church was using a Liturgy of the same family, but with some minor differences, and it seems probable that he would adhere mainly to that to which he and his monks were accustomed, seeing that his English converts would have no preference for one above another.

Gregory's decisions on the laws of marriage are liable to dispute. It is curious to find that people were puzzled then, as some people still are, by the problem whether two brothers may marry two sisters. Gregory's answer is perfectly right — "There is nothing in Scripture against it." Let A and B be the two brothers, and X and Y the two sisters. If A marry X, then B, who is A's brother, is also X's brother, because A and X have become one, but there is no relationship between B and Y; therefore B and Y may lawfully marry.

In the second case, Gregory decides that cousins may not marry, and quotes Scripture as prohibiting it; but all the prohibitions in the chapter from which he quotes are within the third degree of relationship, and cousinship is in the fourth degree; therefore by the divine law, as well as the law of the Empire, cousins might marry. Gregory reckons cousinship in the second degree; but that depends upon the way of reckoning. Gregory reckons by generations:—children are in the first generation and first degree of relationship, cousins in the second generation, and therefore in the second degree of relationship. But the Bible way of reckoning relationship is through the common ancestor, each step up and down being counted. Thus, A is the father of

B and C, D and E are the children of B and C respectively; then to reckon the relationship between D and E, D to B is one step, B to A a second, A to C a third, and C to E a fourth; therefore D and E are outside the forbidden degree.

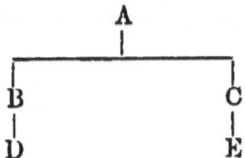

His error is the beginning of the fashion of multiplying disabilities, which reached such a height at last that it necessitated a multitude of dispensations, and made the way for a multitude of divorces, on the ground that the marriage had been within forbidden degrees, and therefore null and void from the beginning.

The prohibition of a man's marriage with his stepmother or his deceased wife's sister is of course scriptural; what needs remark is that Gregory seems at first sight to say that they who contract such marriages before conversion are not to be deprived of holy communion on account of them; as if the Church connived at the violation of its laws. But what he probably means is that the unlawful connection is to be broken off, but that those who entered into it are not to be subjected to a long period of penitential abstinence from holy communion such as would be prescribed to a Christian who should so break the divine law.

The decision on consecration is sound and sensible. The canon of the Council of Nicæa directed that three bishops should assist at a consecration, for the honour of the rite, and for the greater security of its validity; but the Church has always held that consecration by one bishop is valid. What Gregory says is, that where no more are to be had, as in Augustine's circumstances, he need have no conscientious scruple about consecrating alone.

A rather remarkable passage in this letter, in which Gregory speaks of a visit of Augustine to Gaul, and contemplates his acting in consort with Virgilius of Arles, in the correction of abuses among the clergy there, is made more important by the fact that there exists a letter to Virgilius on the same subject. He says to Virgilius: "If our common brother, Bishop Augustine, shall happen to come to you, I desire that your love will, as is becoming, receive him so kindly and affectionately that he may be supported by the honour of your consolation, and others be informed how brotherly love is to be cultivated. And since it often happens that those who are at a distance sooner than others understand the things that need correction, if any crimes of priest or others shall be laid before you, you will, in conjunction with him, sharply inquire into the same. And do you both act so strictly and carefully against those things which offend God and provoke His wrath, that, for the amendment of others, the punishment may fall upon the guilty, and the innocent may not suffer an ill name."—Dated June 22, 601 A.D.

The suggestion to one bishop to interfere with another bishop's discipline over his clergy, and to the latter bishop to admit the interference, seems strange. We are inclined to suspect that in the phrase, "the crimes of priests, *or others*," Gregory means priests or bishops, and that the particular crime he has in mind is that of simony. We know from the History of Gregory of Tours, that the wealthy and powerful bishoprics of Gaul were beginning to be sought by Franks, and the Frank kings were beginning to nominate to them men totally unfit, as rewards for service or gifts of favour, and that gross simony was becoming common. Gregory had much at heart at this time to get a Gallic synod summoned under the presidency of Syagrius, to correct these abuses; it seems probable that he had sent some verbal communication to Augustine as to his possible assistance in the matter, and that the letter to Virgilius was to inform him that Augustine had Gregory's authority for co-operating with him.

On what ground Gregory took upon himself to place under Augustine's authority the British bishops, whose position was quite as independent as that of the Gallican bishops, he does not explain; and the question will be more conveniently considered further on, when Augustine took steps to act upon this direction.

CHAPTER XI

Establishment of the Church in Canterbury

The conversion of Ethelbert had not taken place till some time after the date of Gregory's letter to Bertha, the internal evidence of which assigns it to the year 597 A.D., and it took place some time before the letter to Ethelbert, which is dated 22nd June, A.D. 601. We are disposed to place it sooner rather than later, within these limits.

The work of the Church, consolidated and stimulated by its possession of the completed episcopal constitution, and encouraged by the very striking success indicated by the baptism of the ten thousand, would naturally be prosecuted with hopeful energy. From the first it had the sympathy of the King, or he would not at once have given the missionaries permission to preach and make proselytes. We can easily imagine the influences which would be brought to bear upon him—the teachings of Augustine, added to those of Liudhard, the powerful influence of Bertha; and we can believe that he had abandoned his old religion and its practice for some time before he took the final step of declaring his conversion, and submitting to baptism. The King had to think of the opinions of his chiefs and counsellors, and of the disposition of the mass of his people; and to give them time to reconcile themselves to the idea of the new order of things. It does not appear that Ethelbert took the step which King Edwin afterwards took in Northumbria, of formally submitting the question of a general change of religion to discussion in the Witan. But the conversations between the King and Queen and the two bishops would often take place in the King's hall, in the hearing of those who sat at the royal board; and whenever the King finally declared himself convinced, we may be sure that others of his thanes and knights and wise men would be ready to declare their concurrence in his convictions; and when the King was baptized in the Church of St. Martin, they would follow him to the font. That Whitsunday was chosen for the great ceremony, as the monkish historians affirm, may be accepted as true, and that it was the Whitsunday of 598 is a probable statement. Bede expressly says that "after the King believed and was baptized, greater numbers flocked together daily to hear the Word, and, forsaking their heathen rites, were joined to the unity of the Church"; and that "the King so far encouraged their conversion, that, while he compelled none to embrace Christianity, he showed more affection to the believers, as to his fellow-citizens in the heavenly kingdom."

Then we enter upon the history of the measures which the King took on behalf of the Church. Among other things, he allowed Augustine "to build and repair churches in all places." The mediæval monks of St. Augustine's say that, as a first step, Ethelbert gave to Augustine a building in which he had been accustomed to practise heathen worship, situated between the east wall of the city and the Church of St. Martin, and that Augustine turned it into a church, and dedicated it to St. Pancratius. The reason given by Thomas of Elmham for this dedication is, because it was the sight of the English boys in the Roman Forum which caused Gregory to undertake the mission to England, and that Gregory's Monastery of St. Andrew's was built upon the patrimony of St. Pancratius, the popular boy saint of Rome. We know how exiles of all times fondly give to their new settlements the names of their old homes; it is interesting to recognise the feeling in the hearts of these Roman exiles. Their first monastary they dedicate to SS. Peter and Paul, the patron saints of Rome, and the church at Rochester to St. Andrew, and this chapel to St. Pancras.

We learn from Bede's trustworthy History that Ethelbert "gave his teachers a settled residence in his Metropolis of Canterbury, with such possessions of different kinds as were necessary for their subsistence." Hitherto they had had their temporary lodging in the building in the Stable Gate, now they had a settled residence assigned to them. Thorn says that the King gave them his own palace and went to reside at Reculver, where he built himself a new house out of the Roman material which lay ready to use in that ancient Roman town. The mediæval monk appears to be trying to establish a parallel with the legendary story that Constantine on his conversion gave up his palace to the Pope, and left him ruler in Rome while he went and built himself a new capital at Constantinople; but as the latter story is contrary to the facts, so the former is unsupported and not very probable. Hitherto the King's officers had supplied the strangers with what they needed; now the King endowed them with such possessions as were necessary. In those days the only way to endow a man or a corporation of men with the things necessary for their subsistence, was to give them land; the " possessions of different kinds " may be an obscure statement of what we know was the case in other early ecclesiastical endowments in Kent; that, together with cultivated land in the east, there went a portion of the forest land in the west and of the marsh land in the south. It is the first instance of the endowment of the English—as distinguished from the British—Church. It was probably at the same time that Ethelbert gave to Augustine "a church which he was informed had been built by the ancient Roman Christians, which he reconstructed by the name of Christ Church, and there established a residence for himself and for his successors." We gather that the house given to Augustine and his monks adjoined or was in the immediate neighbourhood of this ancient church.

We have the great good fortune to possess information enough to enable us, with considerable completeness and accuracy, to restore this ancient church; and this is the more interesting, because it is the solitary instance (if we except the doubtful case of Brixworth, North Hants) in which we can recover in its entirety a church of the Roman British period.

The description of the building occurs in the account by Eadmer, the chanter, of a fire which greatly damaged the interior in 1067 A.D. Omitting details which belong to a later time, this is his description :—
" This is that very church which had been built by the Romans, as Bede bears witness, which was arranged in some measure (*in quadam parte*) in imitation of the blessed Prince of the Apostles, Peter." Under the

east end was "a crypt, which the Romans call a Confession, the upper part of which rose above the level of the choir of the singers by several steps. . . This crypt was made beneath in the likeness of the confession of St. Peter, the vault of which was raised so high that the part above could only be reached by many steps. . . Thence the choir of the singers was extended westward into the body (*aula*) of the church, and shut out from the multitude by a suitable enclosure. . . . In the next place, beyond the middle of the length of the body, there were two towers which projected beyond the aisles of the church. The south tower had an altar in the midst of it, which was dedicated in honour of the blessed Pope Gregory. At the side was the principal door of the church, which, as of old, by the English was called the *Suthdure*, and is often mentioned by this name in the law books of the ancient kings [1]; for all disputes from the whole kingdom which cannot be legally referred to the King's Court or to the Hundreds or Counties do in this place receive judgment. Opposite to this tower, and on the north, another tower was built in honour of the blessed Martin, and had about it cloisters for the use of the monks. And as the first tower was devoted to legal contentions and judgments of this world, so in the second the younger brethren were instructed in the knowledge of the offices of the Church, for the different seasons and hours of day and night.

The extremity of the church was adorned by the oratory of the Blessed Mother of God, which was so constructed that access could only be had to it by steps. At its eastern part there was an altar, consecrated to

---

[1] See a learned legal disquisition by Selden, *Dec. Script.* p. 42.

THE CHURCH ESTABLISHED IN CANTERBURY 81

the veneration of that Lady, which had within it the heart of the blessed virgin Austroberta. When the priest performed the divine mysteries at the altar, he had his face turned to the east towards the people, who stood below. Behind him to the west was the pontifical chair, constructed with handsome workmanship, of

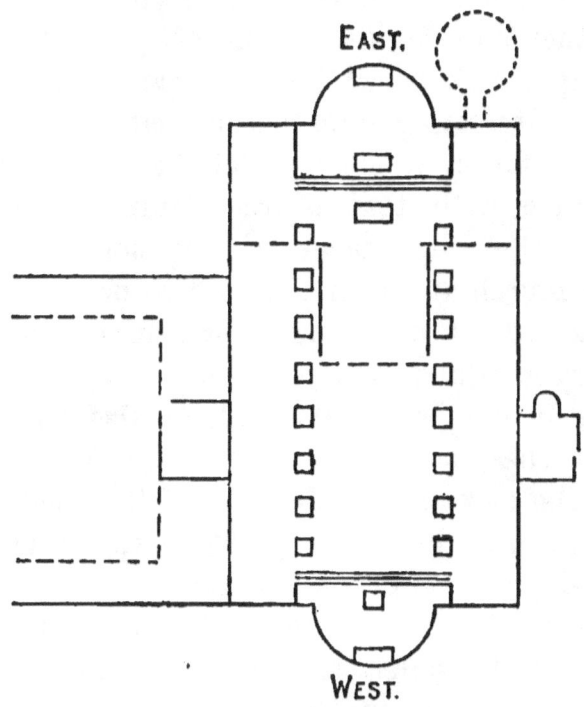

Baptistery added by Archbishop Cuthbert.

large stones and cement, and far removed from the Lord's Table, being contiguous to the wall of the church, which embraced the entire area of the building."

Later on we find that "the pillars of the interior of the church" were greatly injured by the fire.

The building, therefore, was of the basilican type,

with a body and aisles separated by two rows of pillars. Whether these pillars carried a horizontal architrave, or a series of arches, we cannot be sure, but more probably the latter. It had the remarkable feature of a western as well as an eastern apse; the same feature appears at Trier, and only in three or four other churches in the Rhine country, viz. Bemburg, Rothenburg, Mainz, and Laach. The floor of the eastern apse was raised by the crypt beneath; and it is very interesting information that this crypt was made in imitation of the crypt of the old St. Peter's at Rome, which, with that of St. Paul, was the great object of the pilgrimages of the northern nations. Wilfrid's church at Ripon was said to have been built upon the site of an ancient British church, and has also a crypt, which was perhaps a copy of the same venerable confession; and Hexham, also one of Wilfrid's churches, has a similar crypt. What was the cause of the elevation of the floor of the western apse we are not told; but it is probable that there also it was occasioned by a crypt.

In Eadmer's time there were altars at the east end; one built against the wall of rough stones and mortar by Archbishop Odo, to contain the body of Archbishop Wilfrid of York, which he had translated to Canterbury; and afterwards another altar was placed at a convenient distance before the aforesaid altar, and dedicated in honour of our Lord Jesus Christ, at which the divine mysteries (in Eadmer's time) were duly celebrated. But the archbishop's throne was a handsome stone construction, placed in the middle of the semicircular wall of the western apse, and the original altar would be placed before it on the chord of the apse, as at the Lateran and at St. Peter's; and the celebrant would face eastward, as Eadmer expressly says. The choir was an elevated platform, carried out from the chord of the eastern apse into the nave, and divided from the nave by stone screens.

All this is exactly the normal plan of a basilican church, with two exceptions, one the western apse, and the other the consequence of it, that since the usual entrance on the west was prevented by the existence of the apse, the principal entrance was placed on the south, and was known as the *Suthdure* (the south door); apparently the entrance was through the south tower door, whose lower storey formed a porch to it. These flanking towers are not usual in the ordinary basilican church, but they are not without parallel. The sixth-century Church of St. Apollinare in Classe, Ravenna, has a lateral tower. There is a tower at Rochester of earlier date than the present cathedral, which probably occupied a similar position in relation to the coeval church. Exeter Cathedral has two Norman lateral towers. The use of the south tower at Canterbury as a legal court is very interesting. Was the chamber of the tower used as a record office for the documents of the court? In mediæval times the south porches of churches and the chambers over them were sometimes similarly used.

Eadmer speaks of the cloister as if it were a part of the work of Augustine in adapting the Roman Church to the uses of his mission; the monastic life almost necessitated the usual buildings—chapter-house, refectory, day-room, dormitory, arranged round a cloister court. They may have been at first of timber only, as the majority of the Saxon monasteries were, or Augustine may have found more substantial material in the débris of the ruined Roman buildings, as Saxon and mediæval builders did in Colchester and other Roman cities.

This reconstruction of the building helps us greatly in the endeavour to picture the scene at a service:— the tall form of Augustine seated in his handsome stone chair at the west end, vested in planeta and (to anticipate) pall; his priests on a raised stone bench on his right and left, and the Italian monks with their russet robes and shaven crowns in the choir, singing the service to the new Gregorian chants; the King and Queen in conspicuous places; and the great *aula* of the church filled with countrymen and countrywomen of the English slaves who had touched the great heart of Gregory in the Forum of Rome; all saved *De irâ*, from the wrath of God, and singing the *Alleluia*, which has never since been silent in the land.

During all these proceedings there is nothing said of Bishop Liudhard; and yet he must have taken a conspicuous part. Even if he restricted himself to his special duties as chaplain of the Queen and her household, until the consecration of Augustine, the bishop must have celebrated mass in the Queen's Chapel of St. Martin's. It would be unnatural if both the Queen and her bishop failed to take the liveliest interest in what was going on, and to give such assistance as their position enabled them to give. There existed no such hindrances to cordial co-operation between Liudhard and Augustine as we shall find did exist between Augustine and the British bishops. We may perhaps account for the silence about him on the ground of the brevity of the narrative, and the fact that Augustine was its hero. It is possible that, as soon as Augustine was made bishop of the now Christian court and kingdom, Liudhard's services being no longer necessary, he returned to Gaul; but it is much more likely that he continued to act as the Queen's chaplain and director of her household (see p. 164); the ancient tradition is that he died at Canterbury, and was buried in the Church of SS. Peter and Paul. In the Middle Ages the monastery claimed to possess his relics, which were preserved in a golden shrine in the sanctuary, and carried in procession on Rogation days. There is another tradition, that from the time of Augustine to that of Lanfranc, there was a series of suffragan Bishops of St. Martin's, which seems to point to the continuance of Liudhard at St. Martin's, after Augustine had restored Christ Church, and set up his See in it.

CHAPTER XII

THE ARRIVAL OF THE SECOND BODY OF MISSIONERS

WITH a Christian King and Queen at court, with a bishop and a strong staff of ecclesiastics established in their permanent home in the capital, and with a cathedral church in which the divine worship was presented with solemn dignity and beauty, the Church of the English nation began to present an imposing appearance to the world about it, and the number of converts rapidly increased. Our own recent experience has given us occasion to note, with some degree of reverent wonder, the practical effects of the introduction of the episcopate among a handful of missionaries, and the accelerated success of a completely organised Church. The conversions were natural and spontaneous, for Bede expressly says that the King " had learned from his instructors and guides to salvation that the service of Christ ought to be voluntary, not by compulsion." But throughout the history of the English conversion we find the people ready to follow the example of their natural leaders; and while the princes did not persecute Christianity, but readily embraced it, so they did not exercise any compulsion upon the people to embrace it, but only set them a good example.

So great was the success in the succeeding years,

that in the year 601 A.D., Augustine sent Laurence the Priest to Rome to report progress, and to ask for a reinforcement of men, since the harvest was so great that there were not labourers to gather it. The great Bishop responded to the appeal, and resolved to send a second group of monks and clerks. How many we are not told, but Bede gives the names of the principal men among them, Mellitus, Justus, Paulinus, and Rufinianus.

Of the thirty or forty men who formed the original mission staff only three are known by name—Laurence, who succeeded Augustine in the See; Peter, who was made the first Abbot of St. Augustine's Monastery; and Honorius, the fifth and last of the Italian dynasty. Of the new body of men now sent, Mellitus was an abbot to begin with, probably the Abbot of Gregory's Monastery of St. Andrew, and he was soon after sent as bishop to London, Justus to Rochester, Paulinus to Northumbria, and Rufinianus was the third Abbot of St. Augustine's Monastery. We conclude that the original body of men were pious, earnest monks, admirable in the cloister; but that there was a lack of men of "light and leading" among them; and that on a hint from Augustine, or seeing the position of things for himself, Gregory had sent him some men of higher type, capable of initiating, leading, organising, impressing their personality upon others.

It must be borne in mind, in justice to the monks, that the majority of them were probably laymen, with no pretension to be theologians or preachers or missioners in any other sense than that of showing the example of what was then considered to be the highest phase of the Christian life.

The wise Bishop took the same care as before to make the journey of the new band easy, by furnishing them with letters of introduction all along their route. Among the Letters of St. Gregory we find letters to Mennas of Telona (Toulon), Serenus of Massilia (Marseilles), Virgilius of Arelate (Arles), Arigius of Vapincum (Gap), Lupus of Cabillonum (Chalons-sur-Saone), Ætherius of Lugdunum (Lyons), Desiderius of Augustodunum (Autun), Aigulfus of Mettæ (Metz), Simplicius of the Parisii (Paris), Melantius of Rotomagus (Rouen), and Licinius [of Andegavum (Angers) ?].

A selection from these names carries us, as before, from Marseilles up the Rhone and Saône, then to Paris, and so down the Seine to Rouen; but it is difficult to account for some of the other places. Toulon indeed was on the road from Marseilles or Arles to Lerins, whose famous monastery was visited by Augustine in his first journey. But Gap lies a hundred miles to the east of the Rhone, up among the Alps. Metz was still further out of their way, but it was the usual residence of Theodebert the Austrasian King, as Chalons was of Theodoric. Angers lies hundreds of miles away in the west, but it is to be noticed that Gregory's letter is addressed to Licinius without the designation of any place, and though Licinius was about that time Bishop of Angers, it is possible that he was not there at that time. On the whole, we are inclined to assume that the route was that which is above suggested, by the Rhone, Saône, and Seine; and this is supported by the fact that there is this time—there was not on the first journey—a letter to Clothaire the King of Neustria, the western division of the Frank dominions. It must be noted also that one of the letters is addressed to a group of bishops, namely, those of Toulon, Marseilles, Chalon, Metz, Paris, Rouen, and (Angers?); but probably there were separate copies of it addressed to each.

There are two subjects dealt with in most of these letters. Gregory was very desirous of getting the Frank sovereigns and the bishops with whom he was in correspondence to use their influence to summon a synod of the Gallican Church, to take measures against the simony and other abuses which were a mischief and scandal. He takes this opportunity to urge the matter. That he did not succeed is an illustration of the absence of authority and even the limited influence of the See of Rome in the Gallican Church at that time, even when filled by a man of so great personal qualities as those which commended Gregory to the admiration and respect of the Churches. The other topic of the letters is the commendation of Laurence and Mellitus to the good offices of his correspondents.

It will be sufficient to give the substance of the "circular letter," which is limited to the one subject which specially concerns this history.

He says: "Though the duty of your office admonishes your Fraternity to aid religious men, and especially those who are labouring for the good of souls, yet it is not superfluous that our letters should stimulate your solicitude, because, as fire is increased when fanned by a breeze, so the earnestness of a good mind is augmented by commendation.

"Since, therefore, by the co-operation of the grace of our Redeemer, so great a multitude of the nation of the Angles has been converted to the grace of the

Christian faith, that our very reverend brother and fellow-bishop Augustine declares that those who are with him are not sufficient to follow the work into different places, we are sending to him certain monks, with our most beloved and common sons, Laurence the Presbyter and Mellitus the Abbot. Will your Fraternity show them such charity as is proper, and hasten to aid them in whatsoever they may need, that while they may have no cause for delay they may be refreshed by your kindness, and that you may be found partakers in their reward, for your aid in the work in which they are engaged."

The letter to Theodoric, King of the Franks, after exhorting him to summon a synod, goes on to say: "What good things your Excellency did to our very reverend brother and fellow-bishop, as he was journeying to the nation of the Angles, certain monks returning from him have informed us. Wherefore returning abundant thanks, we beg that to the present monks also who are sent to him, you will condescend to give your help still more abundantly, and to assist them on their journey; so that the more your kindnesses are extended to them, so much the more you may receive a greater reward from the Almighty God whom they serve." A letter of similar substance, though differently worded, is sent to Theodebert. Gregory, writing also on this occasion to King Clothaire, tells him that messengers returning from Augustine have informed him what great kindness the King had shown to him on his journey to England, and begs that he will be equally kind to Laurence the Priest and Mellitus the Abbot.

In his letter to Queen Brunhilda, Gregory thanks

God for her love for the Christian religion and the propagation of the truth, and tells her that fame had not been silent about the favour and munificence which she had shown to Augustine when proceeding to England, and that certain monks who returned from England had also related it to Gregory. How many and how great miracles our Redeemer has worked in the conversion of the above-mentioned nation is known to her Excellency, at which she ought to rejoice, because it is partly due to her aid. He goes on to pray that she will the more graciously bestow her patronage upon the monks who are the bearers of these presents (whom he is sending to Augustine, together with his beloved sons Laurence the Priest and Mellitus the Abbot, because Augustine says that those who are with him are not sufficient), so that they may find no difficulties or delays; and tells her that she will the more obtain the mercy of God towards herself and her grandsons who are dear to Gregory, the more she shall for His love show kindness in this matter.

By the hands of these newcomers Gregory sent to Augustine the honorary distinction of the pall, and the tenor of the letter which accompanied it seems to indicate that it was distinctly intended to be a badge of Metropolitan jurisdiction. The letter is as follows:—

> "To his most Reverend and Holy Brother and Fellow-Bishop Augustine — Gregory the Servant of the Servants of God.

"Since it is certain that the unspeakable rewards of the eternal kingdom are reserved for those who labour for Almighty God, yet it is requisite that we bestow upon them the advantage of honours, to the end that they may, by this recompense, be enabled the more vigorously to apply themselves to the care of their spiritual work. And whereas the new Church of the English is, through the goodness of the Lord and your labours, brought to the grace of God, we grant you the use of the pall in the same, for the performance of the solemn service of the mass only; so that you in several places ordain twelve bishops, who shall be subject to your jurisdiction, in such manner that the Bishop of London shall for the future be always consecrated by his own synod, and that he receive the honour of the pall from this Holy and Apostolical See, which I by the grace of God now serve. But we will have you send to the city of York such a bishop as you shall think fit to ordain; yet so that if that city, with the places adjoining, shall receive the Word of God, that bishop shall also ordain twelve bishops and enjoy the honour of a Metropolitan; for we design, if we live, by the favour of God to bestow on him also the pall; and yet we will have him to be subservient to your authority; but after your decease he shall so preside over the bishops whom he shall ordain as to be in no way subject to the jurisdiction of the Bishop of London. But for the future let this distinction be between the bishops of the cities of London and York, that he may have the precedence who shall be first ordained. But let them unanimously dispose, by common advice and uniform consent, whatever is to be done out of zeal for Christ; let them arrange matters with unanimity, decree justly, and perform what they judge convenient in a uniform manner.

" But to you, my brother, shall, by the authority of our God and Lord Jesus Christ, be subject, not only those bishops you shall ordain, and those that shall be ordained by the Bishop of York, but also all the priests [*sacerdotes*, may mean bishops] in Britain ; to the end that from the mouth and lips of your Holiness they may learn the rule of believing rightly and living holily ; and so fulfilling their office in faith and good conduct, they may, when it shall please the Lord, attain the heavenly kingdom. God preserve you in safety, most reverend brother.—Dated the tenth of the Kalends of July [22nd June] in the nineteenth year of our most pious Lord and Emperor, Mauricius Tiberius, the eighteenth year after the consulship of our said Lord, in the fourth indiction [A.D. 601].

CHAPTER XIII

The History of the Pall

The subject of the pall is an important one in the history of our English Church. This ecclesiastical ornament was assuming a new meaning at the period of which we are writing; and the gift of it to Augustine seems the very point at which that new significance was definitely attached to it by the See of Rome, which lasted throughout the mediæval period of the Church's history. It is quite worth while to bestow some time and pains upon it.

About the time of Augustus, the *toga*, which had formed the usual upper garment of a Roman, was superseded in general use by the *pallium*. The pallium was a large oblong piece of woollen fabric, like the robe which some races — as the North American Indians, and the native tribes of South Africa—still wear as their ordinary outer garment; not unlike the plaid the Gaelic inhabitants of the northern part of our own island still use.

It was worn in various ways. Sometimes it was put round the neck, and fastened at the shoulder by a brooch or pin; sometimes passed over the left shoulder, drawn behind the back under the right arm, leaving it at liberty for use, and thrown again over the left shoulder, covering the left arm; sometimes, when it was not needed for warmth or shelter, it was folded twice or thrice lengthwise, and thrown over the shoulder. A man permanently engaged in active occupation would lay aside his pallium altogether. In the old time the officials of the State were distinguished by an embroidered *toga*—*toga picta*, and when the pallium came into general use, an embroidered pallium equally marked out the officials of the Empire.

But the pallium also went out of fashion in its turn, and was succeeded by the *planeta*, a square of woollen material with a slit in the middle, through which the head was passed, and the garment fell in natural folds round the person. It still survives in Spanish South America under the names of *poncho* and *serapé*. About the same time the dalmatic came into use, a garment shaped and fitted to the person, like a short and broad tunic, with short, wide sleeves.

But officialism would no longer follow the vagaries of fashion; a civic dignitary still wore the pallium as a badge of office; only the pall was reduced to its embroidered hem; it was now a long narrow slip of embroidered material, which was worn in a peculiar way about the shoulders. John the Deacon describes it minutely, as it was worn by Bishop Gregory. It was brought round from the right shoulder under the breast, reaching down to the stomach, then up by the left shoulder and thrown behind the back; while the other end, coming over the same shoulder, hung by its own weight down the left side. This exactly describes the pall, as we see it represented in the mosaics of the sixth and later centuries at Rome and Ravenna.

This way of wearing the pall was a preservation of the folds into which the embroidered hem of the old pallium used to fall when it was an actual garment, and continued in use down to the tenth century. About that time the pall was for convenience made up in a large circle, which passed round the shoulders, with two straight pieces sewn on so as to hang down before and behind. It was a much less graceful, but no doubt a much more convenient arrangement, and this continued to be the form of the pall throughout the Middle Ages, and indeed down to the present time.

But how came Bishop Gregory to wear it? The Emperors had been accustomed to give honorary distinctions to those whom they desired to distinguish or to conciliate. In the decay of the Empire, they had conferred the title of Consul and Patrician, not only upon distinguished Romans, but upon Barbarian kings and chiefs; they had bestowed the pallium upon lesser people of various kinds. The Bishop of Rome wore it, either by right as a member of the magistracy of Rome, or it had been granted to the See by some early Emperor. We are told that it was made of byssus, fine flax, or linen, and it appears probable that he wore it on all State occasions. The Bishops of Ravenna also claimed to wear it, by right of a decree from Valentinian—a great benefactor to the Church of Ravenna—and also to wear it on all State occasions. For in the time of Bishop John, Gregory endeavoured to restrict his use of the pall to the time of celebration of the divine service; and when the patrician, the prefect, and many other noble citizens of Ravenna interposed to maintain the privileges of their city, Gregory professed to have satisfied himself by inquiry of Adeodatus, formerly a deacon of Ravenna, that it had been customary for the bishop to wear it only on the occasion of the great "litanies," that is, processions; and he compromised the matter by sanctioning its use on the solemnities of St. John the Baptist, St. Peter, St. Apollinaris (the patron saint of the city), and the anniversary of the bishop's consecration. One of the letters of Gregory to Desiderius, Bishop of Vienne, shows that the bishop of that earliest Church of Gaul had applied for the pall, on the ground that it had been granted to his See in ancient times. That it was the first Christian Church in Gaul, might have been a title to such distinction; Gregory does not dispute the possibility of it, but says that he can find no document relating to it in the record chest (*armarium*) at Rome, and asks Desiderius to cause a search to be made among the records at Vienne.

But how came the Bishops of Rome to confer this distinction upon others? There is a doubtful case of the gift of the pall by Marcus, Bishop of Rome, to the Bishop of Ostia (the official consecrator of the Bishops of Rome) in 336 A.D. But, putting aside this isolated and doubtful case, the custom of the gift of this honorary distinction by the Bishop of Rome to bishops began in the sixth century, and the first instance of it is by Symmachus to Theodore, Archbishop of Laureatus, in Pannonia in 514 A.D. In 523 A.D., Vigilius deferred giving the pall to Auxanius, Bishop of Arles (the ancient capital of Southern Gaul), till he had the Emperor's consent. In 595, at the request of King Childebert, Gregory sent the pall to Virgilius of Arles. In 597, in answer to the request of Queen Brunhilda, for the pall to be given to Syagrius, Bishop of Autun, Gregory replies that it cannot be given without the consent of the Emperor.

The explanation is, that the municipal government of Rome retained the great name of the Senate, and affected to retain the ancient rights of that distinguished body, among them that of conferring the honours of the city upon illustrious strangers; and the Emperors and Gothic kings had been in the habit of allowing these reminiscences of bygone greatness. When the Roman territory threw off its dependence upon the distant Emperor of the East, the Senate distributed these honours without asking his permission. A late remarkable instance of this was when the Senate conferred the title of Patrician upon Pepin and his sons also; and one still more momentous, when, on Christmas Eve of 800 A.D., it assumed to elect Charles as Emperor, and thus to revive the lapsed Empire of the West.

Down to the time of Gregory, the pall was nothing more than a complimentary badge, conferred upon the occupants of some of the most distinguished Sees. Gregory was the first who began to make it a distinctive badge of a Metropolitan, though it was still—down to the present day—sometimes conferred on very distinguished Sees which were not Metropolitan. When Pepin had endowed Rome with his Lombard conquests, and freed it from subjection to the Eastern Emperor, the Popes granted the pall on their own sole authority.

Very soon the conferring of this and similar honours was made use of to help to build up the authority which the See of Rome was usurping over the Christians of the West. In the eighth century the honour of the pall was conferred upon all Metropolitans, and (usually) was limited to them, and was made a token of the formal recognition by the See of Rome of the accession of a new archbishop.

Next, it was claimed by Pope Nicholas I. (A.D. 866), that a new archbishop was not fully made until his appointment had been confirmed by the See of Rome, and that the giving of the pall was the token of this confirmation.

Lastly, in the twelfth century, a new archbishop was required to come to Rome in person (or with special permission to send an agent) to do homage to the See of Rome, and the pall was made a badge of obedience to the See.

Gregory sends the pall to Augustine, to be worn only at the celebration of the divine service, as a token of metropolitical dignity and jurisdiction. The circumstances suggest that the gift of the pall to Augustine, with the expression of an intention to confer it also upon the contemplated Archbishop of York, was the beginning of the idea of limiting it in future to archbishops, and making it a symbol of recognition by the Patriarch of the West. It is to be noted that the Bishop of Rome never sent the badge to bishops of any other than the Western Church; and that the Eastern bishops all wore the omophorion, which in shape is like the early sixth to tenth century form of the pall, and possibly had the same honorary significance.

Gregory's plans for the organisation of the Church of the English show that the accounts which he had received of Augustine's success had filled him with sanguine expectations of the speedy conversion of the whole people; but they indicate that he had received little definite information of the actual condition of the country and its inhabitants. These vague symmetrical plans for the organisation of the whole country into two ecclesiastical provinces, each with its twelve bishops, together with his instructions as to the treatment of the British bishops, seem to imply that Gregory fancied that the English conquest of Britain resembled the Gothic conquest of Italy and the Frank conquest of Gaul; that the conquerors were a homogeneous people, under the rule of Ethelbert the Bretwalda, and that the British bishops were scattered here and there among the conquerors as they were in Italy and France. His idea seems to be a reconstruction of the old Church of the country, with its old chief cities, London and York, as the metropolitan Sees, with the surviving British bishops and their flocks embraced in the new arrangements. He could not have understood that the country was still divided into halves, of which the eastern half was English and the western half British; that the English half was divided into eight independent kingdoms, each of which must be dealt with separately; and that the ecclesiastical organisation must perforce arise out of the national divisions; and he could hardly have realised that the British bishops whom he committed to Augustine's instruction and rule were the bishops of the large and compact population of half the island, still unconquered and still fiercely fighting for independence.

CHAPTER XIV

Gregory's Letters, to Augustine on his Miracles, and to Ethelbert

Bede assigns to this same period another letter to Augustine, which it will be convenient first to put on record, and then to comment upon it. "I know, most loving brother, that Almighty God, by means of your zeal and affection, shows great miracles in the nation which He has chosen. Wherefore, it is necessary that you rejoice with fear, and tremble whilst you rejoice, on account of the same heavenly gift, namely, that you rejoice because the souls of the English are by outward miracles drawn to inward grace; but that you fear lest, amidst the wonders that are wrought, the weak mind may be puffed up in its own presumption, and as it is externally raised to honour, may thence inwardly fall by vainglory. For we must call to mind that when the disciples returned with joy after preaching, and said to their Heavenly Master, 'Lord, in Thy name even devils are subject to us,' they were presently told, 'Rejoice not that the devils are subject to you, but rejoice rather that your names are written in heaven,' etc. . . . It remains, therefore, most dear brother, that amidst those things which, through the working of our Lord, you outwardly perform, you always inwardly judge yourself strictly, and clearly understand both what you are yourself, and how much grace is in that same nation, for the conversion of which you have received the gift of working miracles. And if you remember that you have at any time offended your Creator, either by word or deed, see that you always call it to mind, to the end that the remembrance of your guilt may crush the vanity which rises in your heart. And whatsoever you shall receive or have received in relation to working miracles, see that you consider the same, not as conferred on you, but on those for whose salvation it has been given you."

Gregory does not dispute the miracles. Their occasional occurrence was generally believed; but while the superstitious accepted marvellous stories with ready belief, the wiser minds of the Church had long since taken up a more cautious and critical attitude on the subject. Something in the tone of Augustine's communication of the supposed miracles had roused the fears of his more sober-minded master, that he was, like some of the Corinthians of old (1 Cor. xii. and xiv.), allowing himself to be puffed up with spiritual pride at the possession of this supernatural power. His suggestion is, in the circumstances, admirable, that the miracles are due, not to any superior excellency in him, but to the goodness of the people which calls down these marks of divine favour upon them; the admonition is severe, to take care lest the weak mind be puffed up in its own presumption, and fall through vainglory; and the advice excellent, to crush down the vanity which rises in his heart by calling to mind his sins.

Bede cursorily speaks of miracles as influencing the first conversions among the people; and we shall read in the sequel the details of one miracle by which Augustine attempted to obtain the obedience of the British bishops, and then will be the time to consider the subject a little more closely.

Gregory at the same time sent a letter to King Ethelbert, with very many presents of various kinds.

> "To the most glorious Lord, and his most excellent Son Ædelberet, King of the English—Bishop Gregory.

"The design of Almighty God in advancing good men to the government of nations, is that He may, by their means, bestow the gifts of His mercy on those over whom they are placed. This we know to have been done in the English nation, over whom Your Glory was therefore placed, that, by means of the good things which are granted to you, heavenly benefits might also be conferred on the nation that is subject to you. Therefore, my illustrious son, do you with a careful mind preserve the grace which you have received from the divine goodness, and hasten to promote the Christian faith which you have embraced among the people under your subjection, multiply the zeal of your rectitude in their conversion, suppress the worship of idols, overthrow the structures of the temples, edify the manners of your subjects, and promote great purity of life, by exhorting, terrifying, soothing, and giving examples of good works, that you may find Him your rewarder in heaven, whose name and knowledge you shall spread abroad upon earth. For He also will render the fame of your honour more glorious to posterity, whose honour you seek and maintain among the nations.

"For even so Constantine, our former most pious Emperor, recovering the Roman commonwealth from the perverse worship of idols, subjected the same with himself to our Almighty God and Lord Jesus Christ, and was himself, with the people under his subjection, entirely converted to them. Whence it followed that his praises transcended the fame of former princes, and he as much excelled his predecessors in renown as he did in good works. Now, therefore, let Your Glory hasten to infuse into the kings and people that are subject to you the knowledge of one God—Father, Son, and Holy Ghost—that you may both surpass the ancient kings of your nation in praise and merit, and become by so much the more secure against your own sins before the dreadful judgment of Almighty God, as you shall wipe away the sins of others in your subjects.

"Our very reverend brother Augustine is skilled in the monastic rule, full of the knowledge of the Holy Scripture, and by the help of God endowed with good works; whatever he shall counsel, give ear to, devoutly perform, and carefully keep in memory; for if you give ear to him in what he speaks for Almighty God, the same Almighty God will the sooner hear him praying for you. But if, which God forbid, you slight his words, how shall Almighty God hear him in your behalf whom you neglect to hear for God? Unite yourself, therefore, to him with all your mind in the fervour of faith, and further his endeavours through the help of that strength which the Divinity gives you, that he may make you partaker of His kingdom, whose faith you cause to be received and maintained in your own.

"Besides, we would have Your Glory know, as we

find in the Holy Scripture, that the end of this present world and the kingdom of the saints is about to come, which can never end. But since the end of the world is approaching, many things are at hand which have not previously been, as changes in the atmosphere (*immutationes aeris*), and terrors from heaven, unseasonable tempests, wars, famines, plagues, earthquakes in divers places; all which things will not nevertheless happen in our days, but after our days they will all come to pass. If you, therefore, find any of these things happen in your country, let not your mind be in any way disturbed; for these signs of the end of the world are sent before for this reason, that we may be solicitous for our souls, expecting the hour of death, and be found prepared in good actions to meet our Judge. Thus much, my illustrious son, I have said in few words, to the end that, when the Christian faith shall increase in your kingdom, our discourse to you may also be increased, and we may be permitted to say the more in proportion as joy for the conversion of your nation is multiplied in our mind.

"I have sent some small presents, which will not appear small when received by you with the blessing of the holy Apostle Peter. May Almighty God, therefore, perfect you in that grace of His which He has begun, and prolong your life here through a course of many years, and after a time receive you into the congregation of the heavenly country. May the grace of God preserve Your Excellency in safety.—Dated, etc." [22nd June 601].

The kind of presents which the good Bishop sent to Ethelbert may be inferred from those which he sent to others. To Theodelinda, the orthodox Queen of the Lombards, he sent a collection of sixty-five holy oils, from the lamps which burned before the principal Roman shrines, each in an ampulla, decorated with Scripture subjects; to Queen Brunhilda he sent a key —perhaps two keys, of gold and silver—into the metal of which had been incorporated some filings from the chain of St. Peter. To the Empress Constantina he says that it is not permitted to comply with her request for a portion of the body of St. Peter, but proposes to send her instead a *brandeum in pyxide*, which probably means a napkin which had touched the saintly relic, enclosed in a round ivory box, carved externally with Scripture subjects. Some such things, highly valued by the superstition of the time, probably composed Gregory's presents to the King.

CHAPTER XV

The Beginnings of the Library of the English Church

No doubt the first missionary band brought with them the necessary books and vessels and vestments; but again, with the second band, we are expressly told that Gregory sent all things (*universa*) which were necessary for the worship of the Church, viz. sacred vessels and altar vestments, relics of the apostles and of many saints, and many codices.

Thomas of Elmham describes a number of volumes then preserved in the monastery, some of them placed as relics near the altar, which were believed to have been among those brought to England by Augustine and his companions. He says of them, with pardonable pride, *Hæc sunt primitiæ librarum totius ecclesiæ Anglicanæ.* Among these MSS. were two *Textus Evangeliorum*, which Elmham describes.

There is reason to believe that a copy of the Gospels, preserved in the library of Corpus Christi College, Cambridge, and another, in a similar style of writing, in the Bodleian Library, Oxford, are the two identical volumes described above; not only because they are two of the oldest Latin MSS. written in pure Roman uncials which exist in this country, but also because they contain Anglo-Saxon entries now a thousand years old, which connect them with the Monastery of St. Augustine.

The first of these MSS. was, at the time of the dissolution of the religious houses, preserved by Matthew Parker, afterwards archbishop, and by him given to Corpus Christi College. It is described by the late Professor Westwood[1] as a quarto volume, $9\frac{1}{2}$ inches by $7\frac{1}{2}$, and about $2\frac{1}{4}$ thick. The parchment is thin, the ink of a faded brown, the text is written in fine Roman uncials, in double columns, with twenty-five lines in a page. The book is ornamented with drawings of the highest interest, since they are the most ancient monuments of pictorial art existing in this country. Unfortunately only two leaves of these drawings remain. The first of these occurs opposite the commencement of the Prologue to St. Luke's Gospel. It is divided into twelve compartments, each $1\frac{1}{2}$ inch square, separated from each other by narrow red margins, and the whole enclosed with a narrow border, painted to imitate bluish marble with red veins. The subjects of the twelve drawings are—(1) Christ riding into Jerusalem; (2) The Lord's Supper; (3) Christ praying in Gethsemane; (4) The raising of Lazarus; (5) Jesus washing His disciples' feet; (6) Judas betraying his Lord; (7) Christ seized by the Jews, and Peter cutting off the ear of Malchus; (8) Christ before Caiaphas; (9) Christ led away; (10) Pilate washing his hands; (11) Christ led to judgment; (12) Christ bearing His Cross. They are some of the usual cycle of subjects popular in the sixth century, and are treated in the debased classical style of that period.

[1] *Palæographia Sacra.*

The other drawing in the MS. is a figure of St. Luke seated on a throne, within an elaborately ornamented architectural design, consisting of marble columns supporting a semicircular arch, with a bull in the tympanum. The evangelist is habited in a white tunic and buff-coloured pallium, and holds an open book of his Gospel on his knees. In the open space between the double columns which support the arch are introduced a series of miniatures, smaller than the others, of the following subjects: on one side—(1) The annunciation to Zacharias; (2) The finding in the temple; (3) Christ teaching from the boat; (4) Peter worshipping Christ; (5) The resurrection of the widow's son; (6) The call of Matthew. On the other side—(1) Christ answering the doctors in the temple; (2) The healing of the woman who touched the hem of His garment; (3) Christ cursing the barren fig-tree; (4) Christ healing the dropsy; (5) Zaccheus in the tree.

The Bodleian volume is 10 inches by $7\frac{1}{4}$, written in double columns, with twenty-nine lines in a page; the vellum thin and polished; the ink faded and brown; there are no miniatures.

Thomas of Elmham adds: "We have also the Bible of St. Gregory and his Book of the Gospels, and some ancient codices, all which Gregory sent to Augustine."

Leland saw and describes these Gospels as written in majuscule Roman letters, after the manner of the ancients, carrying in their venerable appearance an incredible majesty of antiquity.

Wanley contended that this large Gregorian Bible was alluded to as still existing, in a petition addressed, in 1604, to James I.; and, in the judgment of Professor Westwood, part of this great Bible exists in the British Museum: Royal MS. 1, E. vi.[1]

Mr. Stevenson has, on the contrary, declared that, "with respect to the claims of particular volumes to form part of this donation, the external evidence is dubious, and the internal evidence condemnatory"; while Mr. Hardwick, the editor of *Elmham* in the *Rolls Series*, says: "With regard to the Corpus MS., enough, I think, might be advanced to make it probable that we have here at least one veritable relic of St. Gregory's benefaction."

[1] *Archæological Journal*, xl. 292.

CHAPTER XVI

THE OLD TEMPLES AND CHURCHES

ANOTHER letter from Gregory to Abbot Mellitus comes in here in chronological order; it is dated June 17, 601; but the internal evidence seems to prove that it was sent at least some months after the departure of Laurence, Mellitus, and the company of monks whom they conducted, for it begins by saying: "We have been much concerned since the departure of our congregation which is with you, because we have received no account of the success of your journey." The batch of letters sent by Mellitus, for instance that to Augustine granting the pall, and that to Ethelbert, are dated the 22nd of June 601. The journey of the party to England would occupy some months, and that of a messenger back with tidings of their safe arrival not much less time, and it might be expected that there would be some interval before the messenger was sent off, and another interval before Gregory would begin to be anxious at not receiving news; so that it might well be a twelvemonth before the letter would be sent to Mellitus. It is certainly the latest extant letter of Gregory on the subject of the English mission, and its date might very likely be June 602.

The interest of the letter consists in the directions which it contains to Augustine on the details of his mission work. It proceeds: "When, therefore, Almighty God shall bring you to our brother, the Most Reverend Bishop Augustine, tell him what I have, on mature deliberation on the affair of the English, determined upon, viz. that the temples of the idols in that nation ought not to be destroyed [in the letter to Ethelbert he had said, "Suppress the worship of idols, overthrow the temples," so that this order is an afterthought, after "mature deliberation"], but let the idols that are in them be destroyed; let holy water be made and sprinkled in the said temples, let altars be erected and relics placed. For if those temples are well built, it is requisite that they be converted from the worship of devils to the service of the true God; that the nations seeing that their temples are not destroyed, may remove error from their hearts, and, knowing and adoring the true God, may the more familiarly resort to the places to which they have been accustomed. And because they have been accustomed to slaughter many oxen in the sacrifices to devils, some solemnity must be exchanged for them on this account, so that on the day of the dedication, or the nativities of the holy martyrs, whose relics are there deposited, they may build themselves huts of the boughs of trees about those churches which have been turned to that use from temples, and celebrate the solemnity with religious feasting, and no more offer beasts to the devil, but kill cattle to the praise of God in their eating, and return thanks to the Giver of all things for their sustenance; to the end that, while some gratifications are permitted to them, they may the more easily consent to the inward consolations of the grace of God. For there is no doubt that it is impossible to efface everything at once from their obdurate minds; because he who endeavours to ascend to a very high place, rises by degrees or steps, and not by bounds. . . . This it behoves your Affection to communicate to our aforesaid brother, that he, being there present, may consider how he is to order all things."

We need not discuss the policy of utilising the religious sentiment and habits of the converted peoples by elevating and Christianising them; this had always been the policy of the Church. What we have to remark is that the letter contains probably another instance of Gregory's ignorance of the actual condition of the English people; the temples to which he alludes are clearly those in which he supposes that the English people worshipped before their conversion to Christianity.

But it is very doubtful whether they had any "well-built" temples such as Gregory supposed, suitable for conversion into churches. The probability is that the worship of the Teutonic Barbarians was an open-air worship; not a daily or weekly worship like that which our religious customs suggest to us, but an occasional meeting of a tribe or of the inhabitants of a wide district, three or four times a year, at some sacred central place of meeting.

We are told, indeed, that Ethelbert, before his conversion, had been accustomed to worship in a building situated outside the city, between the old Church of St. Martin and the city wall, which Augustine afterwards consecrated as a church, and dedicated to St. Pancratius; but this occurs in a late and doubtful legend.

Ethelbert had given Augustine permission to repair and build churches everywhere, and we have seen there were two of the old British churches still standing at Canterbury, one within and the other without the city, and it is a question of great interest whether there were any others in Kent.

There are several other Roman remains in Kent, which we cannot affirm to have been originally churches of the Romano-British period, but which were incorporated in churches of the Saxon period, and should be studied by anyone who desires to have before his mind a picture of the Kent of Ethelbert and Augustine.

At the north-east corner of the mainland of Kent was the Roman town of Regulbium, part of the enclosure-wall of which remains, and many Roman antiquities have been found within it. Ethelbert is said to have had a residence here, and the estate of Cistêlet, which was his first donation to the Abbey of SS. Peter and Paul, was situated in this neighbourhood. In mediæval times, and down to a recent period, there was a large church here; but the population had departed, the church fell into decay, and a few years ago it was taken down, with the exception of two western towers, which, having long served as a landmark to ships entering the Thames, were preserved to continue their usefulness. Fortunately a local antiquary made careful drawings of a portion of the church, the destruction of which is greatly to be regretted. The nave was separated from the chancel by three round arches, of which the middle one was the same height but rather wider than the side arches; it was supported by two stone columns of rather peculiar design; the shafts tapered slightly from bottom to top (it was not an *entasis*); the bases were ornamented with two or three rows of cable moulding; the composition of the capitals was as if three thin slices of truncated cones had been placed one on the top of the other, with the larger face upwards, and suggested the possibility of the stone capital being merely the block round which mouldings or coronals of metal might have been placed. The arches were turned with Roman brick. The side arches rested upon jambs built of hewn stone with bonding courses of brick at intervals, *more Romano*. These jamb-walls were returned for a yard or two eastward, and then continued by more modern masonry to complete the north and south walls of the chancel. This interesting fragment was probably of late Roman date, say the fifth or sixth century; it might even have been of Saxon date, built out of the materials of the ruined Roman buildings of Regulbium. What use the building of which it formed part had originally served it is difficult to conjecture. A triplet like that did not form part of a colonnade separating a body from its aisle; we have no example of such a triplet between the nave and apse of a basilican church; and if the reader chooses to think that it was the original chancel arch of a church built by Ethelbert adjoining his palace at Reculver, it would be difficult to prove him mistaken.

The double monastery which Ethelburga, the widow of Edwin of Northumbria, founded on her return to Kent in 633 at Lyminge, was built upon the remains of an earlier building, whose foundations still remain; these were considered by the members of the Archæological Institute to represent a Roman residence, including a Christian church, and to belong to the close of the fourth or beginning of the fifth century.

There is a church in Dover Castle, built in large part of Roman bricks, and in the Romanesque style which obtained from the sixth to the twelfth century, so that it is difficult to determine its date. Some antiquaries think it a church of Roman-British times, restored in Saxon times. Others—among them Professor Freeman and Sir G. G. Scott—attribute it to the time of King Ethelbald.

Thus we get a list of more or less probable remains of churches of the old British Church remaining in Kent at the time of the English conversion, viz. St. Martin's and Christ Church, the doubtful castle chapel at Dover, the possible church at Richborough, and the probable foundations at Lyminge.

CHAPTER XVII

The Foundation of the Monastery of SS. Peter and Paul.

The arrival of the new band of missionaries, with men of superior ability among them like Mellitus, Justus, Paulinus, and Rufinianus, would give a great impulse to the good work which was making such progress in the Kingdom of Kent. We are inclined to assign to this period the foundation of the new monastery outside the city of Canterbury. We are not expressly told, but it is reasonable to suppose, that among the English converts to the faith some would be moved to adopt the life which was put before them, by precept and example, as the highest phase of the religious life, that of the cloister; and we conclude that by this time there were English inmates of Gregory's Monastery of Christ Church. The arrival of the new reinforcements would naturally lead to a general consideration of the situation of things, and the formation of new plans for the future. In this new arrangement it was natural that a distinction should be made between those who were monks, desirous of and perhaps only fitted for the life of seclusion, and those whose aims and qualities fitted them for the more active work of evangelisation. It was resolved to found a new monastery for the former, while the latter continued in the city as the missionary staff of the bishop.

Ethelbert gave a site for the new monastery on a plot of ground between the city walls and the old Church of St. Martin. The later monastic historians say that it was the site on which Ethelbert had been accustomed to worship in his unconverted days; that is, the Teutonic place of worship of the people of Canterbury. Thorn says, also, that there was a building there which, on Ethelbert's conversion, Augustine had consecrated as a church, under the name of St. Pancratius; but all this is matter of doubtful tradition. The ruins of a small Chapel of St. Pancras (thirty feet by twenty-five) still exist within the precincts of the cemetery of St. Augustine's Monastery, in the walls of which many Roman bricks have been used, and the arch of a round-headed door is turned with them, but the building is probably of not earlier date than the twelfth century.

What is certain is, that Ethelbert gave the ground, and that Augustine planned a monastery there on a grand scale. It was intended from the first to be the burial-place of the kings and of the archbishops; the kings were to be buried in the south *porticus*, and the archbishops in the north *porticus*. The word *porticus* usually means portico or porch, but Professor Willis is of opinion that what is said of these *portici* makes it necessary to suppose that they were of the nature of transepts. So that the two *portici* were in fact two great mortuary chapels, opening perhaps into the church, in which the sarcophagi of the kings and archbishops would be ranged in order. We call to mind that the building called the Church of SS.

Nazaro e Celso at Ravenna, was in fact a mortuary chapel, built by the Empress Galla Placidia, in which the sarcophagi of herself, her husband Constantius, and her son Valentinian still remain, and that the Bishops of Rome of the third century were buried in a sepulchral chamber appropriated to them, and we suppose that it was the custom of the time to construct such special buildings for the reception of the tombs of great personages. It may be noted here in a parenthesis, that the royal persons who are recorded to have been buried in the south porticus, in accordance with this intention, were King Ethelbert and Queen Bertha, his son King Eadbald and Queen Emma, his son King Ercombert, King Hlothære and his daughter St. Mildred, Mulus, a stranger king who was brother of Cadwalla, and King Withred. The archbishops who were buried in the north porticus were Augustine, Laurence, Mellitus, Justus, Honorius, Deusdedit; in the church itself (because the north porticus was full), Theodore, Tatwin, and Nothelm. Cuthbert desired to transfer the burial-place of the bishops to the baptistry (dedicated to St. John the Baptist), which he had built near the east end of the Cathedral of Christ Church, and ordered that his death should be kept secret until after his burial there, in order that the new monastery might not claim his body; his successor Bregwin was also buried at Christ Church; but the next Archbishop, Jaenberht, who had been Abbot of SS. Peter and Paul when Cuthbert broke the ancient custom, and had loudly protested against it, consistently ordered his own burial to be in the chapter-house of the new monastery. A large plot of ground adjoining the monastery was appropriated as the general cemetery of the neighbouring city.

Everything which we know about the monastery tends to prove that the monkish founders, as they supposed themselves, of the Church of the English, intended that this should be a pattern. The monks of a later day call it the *mater primaria* of the monasteries of England. As a matter of history, we know that the Celtic Monastery of Iona was the *mater primaria* of the monasteries of northern England, and that Benedict Biscop, in founding his monasteries at Wearmouth and Jarrow, and Wilfred those at Ripon and Hexham, did not copy the great monastery of Augustine, but went direct to Italy and Gaul for their exemplars.

Some centuries later there was a great and bitter rivalry between the two monasteries, Christ Church, and the later foundation which by that time was known as St. Augustine's. The latter claimed that its founders, Ethelbert the first Christian King, and Augustine the first Archbishop, had concurred in giving to the new monastery the special privilege that it should be entirely free from interference from king or bishop, together with its estates and churches —" in its head and members, within and without," a little *imperium in imperio*. It is only necessary to say, in dealing with this early stage of its history, that though bishop and king designed to make it a great and model institution, there is no satisfactory evidence that they gave it any such exceptional privileges. The first example which can be established by satisfactory evidence of the exemption of a monastery from episcopal jurisdiction, is that of Fulda, at the instigation of Boniface in 751 A.D.; and when the claims of St. Augustine's became the subject of legal investigation, and the charters were submitted in 1181 A.D. to the examination of a commission, consisting of the Bishop of Durham and the Abbot of St. Alban's, the so-called Charter of Ethelbert, exhibited in evidence, turned out to be a document marred by erasures and interlineations, and not validated by signature and seal, and the so-called Charter of Augustine, to be a document which bore the traces of its recent origin on the face of it, in the character of its writing and the nature of its seal.

We are only concerned with these later passages of history inasmuch as they bear upon the earlier period with which we have to do. We conclude that Augustine founded the Monastery of SS. Peter and Paul, as a part of his organisation of the religious life of the Kingdom of Kent in the first place, with ulterior views of its being an exemplar of the monastic institution among the nation of the English; and we do not doubt that he intended to keep it under the authority of the archbishop, and a part of his general work; just as Gregory had dealt with the Monastery of St. Andrew on the Cælian Hill, when he became Bishop of Rome.

Elmham says that the monastery was founded in 597, which seems too early a date; according to Thorn, it was so far advanced that the King and Queen kept Christmas there in 605; we adhere to the opinion that the new foundation was determined upon soon after the arrival of Abbot Mellitus and the reinforcement of the English mission; that it took some time to settle the preliminaries, to obtain the grant of the site, and the endowments in land from the King; to plan and erect the monastic buildings. We assume that the eastern portion of the church would be built and fitted for the celebration of divine service, and that the domestic buildings would be carried on at the same time, and that the new community would not be separated from the rest of Augustine's family till this was done; these things might well fill up the interval between the year 601 A.D. of the arrival of Mellitus and his company, and the invitation of the King and Queen to a great "house-warming" at Christmas 605, by Abbot Peter and his monks. Peter was one of the band of men who accompanied Augustine; that he was one of the ablest of them we conjecture from the fact that he, with Laurence the Priest, was sent back to report in person to Gregory. Again, to anticipate the future history of the monastery in a parenthesis, since it reflects light upon the present, Peter, soon after his appointment, sailed from Gaul on some errand of which we have no knowledge, and was shipwrecked and cast ashore dead in the Bay of Ambleteuse. He was succeeded by John, another of the original band of missionaries; after him came the Rufinianus mentioned among the most distinguished of the second band of missionaries; he by Graciosus, one of the first company; he by Petronius; he by Nathaniel, one of the second company; then, after a vacancy of two years, came Abbot Adrian, the fellow-labourer of Archbishop Theodore, with whom a new era begins.

Of the fabric of this great and famous monastery we are not so fortunate as to have any description, and the remaining buildings of it are of much later

FOUNDATION OF MONASTERY

date, and afford no clue to its earlier construction. It is very possible that the conventual buildings may have been of timber; that was the usual building material of the Saxons, and nearly all the domestic portions of their monasteries were so built.

The church was long in progress; it was probably of masonry, and as grand as Augustine's reminiscence of Italian monasteries, and the skill of native builders, with his plans and suggestions, could make it. The church, which was the principal and ruling feature of the whole design, would be of the basilican type; it was the universal type of the period. It would have the special features of the two transepts, designed for the mortuary chapels of the kings and archbishops. The cloister-court would be placed, as was the universal custom where no difficulties of site prevented, and here there were no such difficulties, on the south side of the nave, in the quadrangle partially defined by the wall of the nave as its north boundary, and the wall of the transept as its east boundary; and the buildings would consist of the day-room and dormitory over it, the refectory and kitchen, the house for the lay-brothers—the workers and servants of the community, perhaps the house for the entertainment of strangers, all arranged round the central open-air cloistered court, which was the nucleus of a monastic house.

It is a transgression centuries beyond the scope of our history, but entirely within its spirit, to note that the site of the venerable Monastery of St. Augustine, with the remains of its mediæval buildings confiscated and ruined at the Reformation of the sixteenth century, have, in our days, through the devotion and munificence of the late Mr. A. J. B. Beresford Hope, been recovered to the church, and converted, with the necessary new buildings, to the purposes of a Missionary College, which has been sending its students through all the world, to extend the English Church which Augustine planted.

It was not only religion which the Italian monks introduced into Kent, but the civilisation of the ancient Empire. There is one important passage in Bede (ii. 5) which bears upon this subject. He says that among other benefits which Ethelbert conferred upon the nation was this, that, " with the counsel of his wise men, he introduced judicial decrees after the Roman model, which, being written in English, were still (in Bede's time) observed by them. Among these, in the first place, he set down what satisfaction should be given by those who should steal anything belonging to the Church, the bishop, or the other clergy—resolving to give protection to those whose doctrine he had embraced." The wise men by whose counsel Ethelbert introduced a code of laws were no doubt the constitutional Witenagemot. We can hardly doubt that the laws after the Roman model which the King introduced, with the consent of his Witan, were suggested by Augustine, and perhaps through Augustine by Gregory himself, who, we remember, had studied the Roman law in his youth, and administered it as Prætor of Rome.

The circumstances of the case make it highly probable, and the probability is increased by the fact that, among the questions which Augustine put to Gregory[1] was one as to the punishment

[1] P. 68.

to be inflicted upon anyone who should steal from the Church, and that the first of Ethelbert's laws relates to the satisfaction which should be given by those who steal anything belonging to the Church and its ministers.

These "Dooms of Ethelbert" seem to have been issued between 597 and 605; they are the first written code of laws of the English race; they indicate that if the King of Kent did not, like Edwin of Northumbria, consult his Witan before he embraced Christianity and allowed the missionaries to convert such of his subjects as chose to listen to them, he did at an early period seek the sanction of that body for the consequent legislation.

One of the first duties of the monks was to teach learning to such of their converts as, by their social station or exceptional abilities, were fit subjects for it. The new monastery would be a model of architecture to the people, its church probably the first and certainly the finest building of stone erected in Kent since the Roman times. In many ways the cultured Italians would introduce the arts and manners of a refined civilisation among the rude Kentish men.

CHAPTER XVIII

The Negotiation with the British Church

We have seen that, when Gregory assumed to place the British bishops under the Metropolitan jurisdiction of Augustine, as Archbishop of the English, he probably supposed that, as was the case in Italy and Gaul, they were the bishops of surviving towns of the old Roman province, standing like islands amidst the English population which had flowed around them; so that, when the English were converted, it would be highly desirable that the bishops of the two races should be united in one ecclesiastical organisation of the whole country. Augustine found the actual condition of things very different from that which Gregory had contemplated, but still he thought it right to enter into communication with the British bishops, and to invite them to accept the plan which Gregory had sketched out, so far as it was possible in the circumstances. We should hardly have expected that the King of Kent would possess sufficient influence among the British to induce their ecclesiastical leaders to consent to entertain the question and to come to confer with Augustine upon it. The chronic war between the two races, the British and the English, was still in progress. In 577 the West Saxons had won a great battle at Deorham, which had given them possession of Bath, Gloucester, Cirencester, and the country round about those towns, and had thus severed the native inhabitants of the peninsula of Cornwall and Devon from their countrymen in Wales. The Saxons were still pressing the rest of the native population westward, but had not yet extended their conquests to the line which they ultimately attained: Cumbria was still independent, and was disputing the advance of the Northumbrian kingdom with varying fortunes; the continuity of the independent country, from the Firth of Solway to the Bristol Channel, was not severed until, in 613, the result of a great battle at Chester drove in a wedge of Mercia between Wales and Cumbria.

The Church of Wales had lately reorganised itself on the lines which have lasted to the present day. Out of the confusion which followed the break-up of the Roman province, the inhabitants of Wales had grouped themselves into four independent kingdoms— Gwynedd, Powys, Menevia, and Gwent—and in each a separate bishopric had been established; Bangor for Gwynedd, Llanelwy (or St. Asaph) for Powys, St. David's for Menevia, and Llandaff for Gwent. The date of the actual foundation of the Sees is not known; but Daniel, the first Bishop of Bangor, died 584 A.D.; St. David died in 601 A.D.; St. Kentigern, the probable founder of St. Asaph, in 612 A.D.; and in the same year also died Dubricius, the founder of Llandaff.

In spite of the political confusion, learning and religion still flourished in Wales. St. David's monastery especially was a great centre, to which not only native Britons, but the Irish also, were coming for instruction and training in the religious life. From his monastery went forth Finian with several companions, whom legendary story calls the Twelve Apostles of Ireland, to effect a great revival of religion in that island.

This was the condition of the Welsh Church, and some of the great men above mentioned were bishops in it, at the time that Ethelbert invited them to conference with Augustine.

If we try to put ourselves in the position of the British ecclesiastical leaders, when the invitation came to them, we shall perhaps be able to conjecture how the proposal would present itself to their minds. They were the present representatives of the Church which had lately spread over the whole province of Britannia; the withdrawal of the imperial authority from the island, the conquest of half their country by Barbarian and heathen tribes, had made no difference in their ecclesiastical relations with, or in their personal feelings towards, the Churches of the Continent in general and of Rome in particular.

They now learnt officially that the Bishop of Rome, the illustrious Gregory, had sent a mission to convert their barbarous enemies; that this mission had succeeded in converting Kent, or at least in securing a firm footing in that kingdom; and they were asked to meet the chief of this mission, who had been consecrated as Bishop of the English, in friendly conference. Why not?

It may help us to further enter into the thoughts and feelings of the British Church, if we call to mind that after the retirement of the Empire from the island, while the people were harassed by the invasions of the Saxon pirates and the incursions of the Picts and Scots, the Church found leisure for the Pelagian controversy, and held the synods at which Germanus and Lupus had come over from Gaul to assist. It illustrates the disturbed state of the country at that very time, if we remember that while Germanus was here there was an incursion of these foreign foes—both Saxons and Picts—and that Germanus, at the request of the people, put himself at the head of their forces, inspired them with courage, and suggested the stratagem which gained them the famous " Alleluia " victory.

We may also bear in mind that at this very time Rome itself was in circumstances not dissimilar from those in which the Britons found themselves. The Roman territory, smaller than that which the unconquered Britons still retained, was surrounded by the Lombards, continually harassed by their incursions, and in danger of being conquered by them; and yet the ecclesiastical life of Rome went on much as usual, and Gregory engaged in political controversy with the Emperor and an ecclesiastical controversy with the Patriarch of Constantinople, administered the business of his See with an unintermittent vigilance, intervened in the affairs of Gaul, and still had leisure to watch over his mission in distant Britain. War may be raging on our frontier, the enemy may be gaining victories and advancing towards us, but the affairs of daily life are not interrupted till the enemy is actually upon us; and the affairs of daily life of ecclesiastics are the moral and spiritual tendance of their people, and the interests of the Church of Christ.

It is not, then, out of the ordinary course of things

that, amidst the break-up of the Empire in Britain, the people should still be discussing theological questions and holding synods about them; or that, while the armed forces of Wales were engaged with the invading Saxons beyond the Severn, St. David and Caradoc should continue to cultivate learning and religion, should be engaged in reorganising the native Church in accordance with the actual political and social changes which were taking place among the people, should be sending forth missionaries to Ireland, and should be willing to enter into communication with Augustine in the interests of religion.

Augustine would represent to them the Church of the West, with which they had always been in full communion and co-operation. Their representatives had been present in the old time at the great Councils of the Western Church, or, if they had not been represented by delegates, they had sent in their acceptance of the decrees of the Councils. There was no reason, so far, why the British should not give a friendly response to an invitation to a conference with the Roman missionary. Rome was to them still, as it had always been, the premier See of Western Christendom, an object of great respect and reverence. Pious Britons for many generations, while it was possible, had made their pilgrimages to "the threshold of the Apostles" at Rome, and nothing had happened to diminish their reverence for it.

Augustine came to them, through the mediation of Ethelbert, King of Kent, as the Archbishop of the English. Well, the Bishop of Rome had undertaken a good work in essaying to convert the Barbarians who had assailed Britain, as other tribes of the Barbarians had successfully assailed and established themselves in other portions of the Empire. They could do no other than wish him success in his mission. The Kingdom of Kent was far away from them and their present interests. It had been established in its corner of Britain for one hundred and fifty years. Men in those days accepted the logic of events as we do in these days; friendly communications with the now Christian King of Kent, the powerful Bretwalda, could hardly bring the Welsh any harm, and might bring them good. There was no reason here either why they should not meet Augustine in friendly conference; and so they met him.

Where was the meeting held? There are several claimants for the honour of having been the place of this interesting historical event. Two seem to have plausible claims. One of these is the Apostles' Oak, in the parish of Abberley, at the junction of the two dioceses of Worcester and Hereford, which seems to correspond with the words of Bede, who describes the place of meeting as near to the end of the West Saxons, or Wiccii, and there is an ancient tradition that this was the place; another is Austre Clive or Aust in Gloucestershire, on the Severn, where the old Roman ferry is said to have crossed the river to Chepstow.

Bede gives the narrative of the proceedings in some detail. Gregory "began by brotherly admonitions to persuade them to preserve Catholic unity, and with him to undertake the common labour of preaching the gospel to the nations"; and then he enumerates some of the particulars in which they differ from the usages of the Roman Church. The principal of these were the time of keeping Easter, the form of the clerical tonsure, some peculiarity in the ordination of bishops, priests, and deacons, a peculiarity in the mode of administering baptism. They had a Liturgy of their own, and a version of the Bible of their own. It is very important to observe that the differences between the two Churches were only such trifling matters as these; in all the great questions of the doctrines of the faith, the organisation and discipline of the Church, they were entirely agreed.

The whole question came up again half a century afterwards, and was fully debated at the Synod of Whitby. Bede reports the speeches on both sides on that occasion at considerable length, and the reader may profitably read the argument as there given.[1]

The main arguments on one side and on the other were these:—The Italians said that their customs were those of the whole Church, and maintained that it was desirable, for the sake of Catholic unity, that the Britons should conform to them. The Britons pleaded that they followed the customs of their spiritual ancestors, which they had received from St. John the Apostle, and they were unwilling to abandon them. It is well to note this belief of the British Church that it derived its descent from St. John; because it is a confirmation of the conclusion at which we arrive from other evidence, that the Church was planted in Britain by Gallic missionaries, the Gallic Church having itself been founded at Vienne and Lyons by Pothinus, Irenæus, and other missionaries, who came from Asia Minor in the middle of the second century.

[1] Bede, *Eccl. Hist.* Book iii. ch. 25.

It is worth while to bestow a little attention upon these special customs in dispute.

The proper time for the observance of the great Easter festival, upon which other great festivals of the Church depended, had been a subject of dispute between the Churches of the East and the West as early as the middle of the second century. When Polycarp the martyr visited Rome about 158 A.D., the two customs came face to face in the different practice of the "Angel of the Church of Smyrna," and of Bishop Anicetus of Rome. It had been the practice of the Asiatics to celebrate the Paschal Supper on the fourteenth day of the first Jewish month, the same day on which the Jews kept the Feast of the Passover; and three days later they kept the Feast of the Resurrection, on whatever day of the week it might happen to fall. Other Churches, having special regard to the fact that the resurrection had taken place on a Sunday, and that the weekly holy day had been altered by the apostles from the Jewish Sabbath to the Lord's Day on that account, held that the yearly Festival of the Resurrection ought also to be held on a Sunday. The Asiatic or *Quartodeciman* practice was traced to St. John and St. Philip, that of the Western Churches to St. Peter and St. Paul. Polycarp and Anicetus agreed that in such a matter a difference of practice might be allowed.

The question was revived about twenty years afterwards, when Victor, the Bishop of Rome, endeavoured to induce the Eastern Churches to conform to the Western practice, and threatened with excommunication those who declined to agree. Polycrates, Bishop of Ephesus, referred the practice of his Church to St. Philip and St. John; Irenæus, by that time Bishop of Lyons, urged that such a question ought not to be made a ground for a breach of communion, inasmuch as a diversity of usages had always been allowed, and such variation in things indifferent served to confirm the argument which might be drawn from the agreement of all Churches as to the essentials of faith. At length, at the Council of Nicæa, it was agreed by all the Churches, for the sake of uniformity, to adopt the Western usage, and to celebrate the great festival on the first Sunday after the first full moon after the vernal equinox. But it required some astronomical science to calculate the day beforehand, and the duty was laid upon the Bishop of Alexandria, as the great centre of the science of the time, to have it calculated, and to send round to the Churches notice of the proper day.

Next, for the convenience of the Churches, methods of calculating the time of Easter by means of tables, such as those at the beginning of our prayer-books, were invented. One method, which is known as the Cycle of Sulpicius Severus, a disciple of St. Martin of Tours, was adopted by the Western Churches; but after a while it was found to be incorrect, and was superseded by the Cycle of Victorius Aquitanus.

The British Church was not, as is supposed, following the *Quartodeciman* practice of St. John; it had accepted the decision of Nicæa, and had adopted the Cycle of Sulpicius Severus; and in its isolation and backwardness had not exchanged it for the more correct Cycle of Victorius when the other Churches did. We have an instance of precisely the same kind at this day. The fact that the astronomical year (the time of the earth's complete circuit round the sun) is not an exact three hundred and sixty-five days, but three hundred and sixty-five and a quarter nearly, had thrown the civil year out of harmony with the real year, to the amount of eleven days. In 1582 the continental nations of Europe agreed to alter the civil year so as to re-establish the correspondence, and to adopt a new cycle (adding a day to every fourth year) so as to maintain it in the future; but England did not adopt the "New Style" till 1752; the Eastern nations have not yet adopted it; so that the Eastern Churches (including Russia) are now reckoning their days by a calendar twelve days later than the Western Churches.

So long as all the members of a national Church adopt the same day, an error on the subject is of no religious importance; but if in the same nation, and still more in the same city, different persons should adopt different days, it would cause undesirable confusion. So long as the British Church and the English Church remained separate, with little intercourse between them, their different Easters might be allowed; but when, as in Northumbria, different churches were adopting different days, and when the confusion reached its climax in the fact that Oswy and his household were celebrating Easter while Eanflæda and her attendants were still in the Lenten Fast, it was time to come to some agreement.

The shape of the tonsure seems a very unimportant matter, but it has some antiquarian interest. The custom of the clerical tonsure arose perhaps from the desire to increase the venerableness of the appearance of the clergy by an artificial baldness; and this distinction of the clergy by head mark was maintained partly for the sake of the respect to be paid to them, partly for disciplinary reasons. The Eastern tonsure shaved the hair back from the forehead, in imitation of frontal baldness; the Western tonsure shaved the crown of the head, in imitation of coronal baldness. The British tonsure differed from both, and there has been much doubt and difficulty about it. The Bishop of Edinburgh (Dr. Dowden) has lately put forward the theory, and produced some evidence in support of it, that in the British tonsure the fore part of the head was partially shaved up to a line running from ear to ear, but leaving a narrow fringe of hair in front; so that in a front view it looked like the Western tonsure, and in a back view no tonsure at all was visible.

The British custom in the consecration of bishops was probably consecration by one bishop. The Council of Nicæa had directed that three bishops should assist at a consecration, for the greater honour of the rite and for greater security of valid and regular succession; but it was never disputed that the consecration of one bishop was a valid consecration. The peculiarity in the administration of baptism was probably by one immersion instead of three.

The British Liturgy was of the family of the Ephesine Liturgy, called by the name of St. John, but in its adoption in Gaul, Spain, and Britain, some small differences were adopted in each country. It is curious that the Ephesine Liturgy was in the fourth century superseded in its own country by that of St. Chrysostom, but survived in these north-western nations of Europe. The British Liturgy is lost, but the Mosarabic (Spanish) form, from which it differed only in some minor details, is still in actual (occasional) use in Spain.

The British version of the Bible was founded on the Old Latin, but is different from Jerome's Vulgate, and is peculiar to itself.

These were the matters, or some of them, on which Augustine and his assistants on one side, and the British bishops on the other, held a "long disputation"; the result of which was that the British "did not comply with the entreaties, exhortations, or rebukes of Augustine and his companions; but preferred their own traditions before all the Churches in the world which in Christ agree among themselves."

Then Augustine made the startling proposal to submit the dispute to divine decision. "Let us," he said, "beg of God, who causes those who are of one mind to dwell in His Father's house, that He will vouchsafe by His heavenly tokens to declare to us which tradition is to be followed. Let some infirm person be brought, and let the faith and practice of those by whose faith he shall be healed, be looked upon as acceptable to God and be followed by all." The adverse party were taken by surprise; a belief in such appeals to the divine arbitration was one of the common superstitions of the age; they did not see their way to refuse it, and it would seem reluctantly consented. "A blind man of the English race was brought, who, having been presented to the priests of the Britons, found no benefit or cure from their ministry. At length Augustine bowed his knees to the Father of our Lord Jesus Christ, praying that the lost sight might be restored to the blind man, so that by the corporeal enlightening of one man the light of spiritual grace might be kindled in the hearts of many of the faithful. Immediately the blind man received sight, and Augustine was declared by all to be the preacher of divine truth."

But the miracle had not the desired effect. "The Britons confessed that it was the true way of righteousness which Augustine taught, but declared that they could not depart from their ancient customs without the consent and leave of their people. They therefore desired that a second synod might be appointed, at which more of their number would be present."

This is the occasion to which we have deferred the general consideration of Augustine's miracles. We have already seen that Augustine is said to have worked miracles in the very beginning of his work in Kent, and that, in reporting his miracles to Gregory, he had given occasion for very sharp rebuke on the spiritual elation which he manifested on account of them. This is the first and only actual example of them which is recorded; for the later stories, related by his fourteenth and fifteenth century panegyrists, are of no historical value.

The belief in contemporary miracles was general throughout the Middle Ages, and still exists in some countries, and we must bear in mind that sincerely religious and good people may still be ignorant and credulous. But, as a matter of historical fact, we note that, as we trace the history of a saint back from his latest panegyrist to contemporary authorities, we find that the list of his miracles often grows; *i.e.*, the later writers have included a number of traditional stories in their narrative, which were not recorded by, and therefore probably not known to, his contemporaries. It is known to students of this branch of ecclesiastical literature, that certain miraculous stories are repeated in the lives of different saints; just as the same deed of valour is attributed to different heroes of romance.

But when we get back to the contemporary histories of saints, we find that, beyond question, some of them believed that they possessed supernatural power, and that their companions believed that they witnessed examples of its exercise. We must bear in mind the tendency of certain minds to regard things out of the common order as supernatural, the tendency of the persons to whom they happen or who are eye-witnesses of them, to unconscious exaggeration of the strangeness of the event, and the certainty that the story would grow as it passed from mouth to mouth. In the case of healings, we must bear in mind the undoubted fact that remarkable sudden cures, of certain classes of diseases, do occur under strong mental excitement, and that the effect of this excitement is greatly increased by the sympathy of an excited crowd, as in times of religious "revivals." So that we may accept it as true that some of these saints did effect cures which seemed to themselves and to the recipients of the cure, and to the spectators, to be miraculous.

But when we stand face to face with this circumstantial account of the restoration of sight to the blind man by Augustine, we feel that it cannot be explained in this way. What are we to think of it? When we examine the narrative, we note that the British bishops are said to have accepted the proposed test, and to have attempted to work the miracle by their prayers; and that they are said to have admitted the reality of the cure in answer to the prayers of Augustine. But we are most of all struck by the fact that the miracle seems somehow to have failed of its effect. The Britons were confounded by it, but practically they declined to accept its evidence. They postponed their decision to a future conference; and at that future conference the evidence of the miracle does not appear to have been alluded to on either side; somehow the Britons ignored it, and Augustine's party felt that it would not help them. What are we to say about it? We may, perhaps, most conveniently return the ambiguous verdict, which is permitted to a Scotch jury, of "Not proven."

The second conference appears to have been held within a short time and at the same place. The Britons sent messengers to summon some of their most learned and influential men, especially from the Monastery of Banchor Iscoed, so called to distinguish it from the other celebrated monastery of the same name on the Menai Strait. This Banchor Iscoed was on the right (east) side of the Dee, about twelve miles from Chester. Augustine would naturally occupy the interval in trying to make some good impression upon the South Saxon men among whom he found himself.

Both parties had thought over the situation, and had adopted a policy. Augustine had resolved to reduce his demand for an abandonment of the old

British customs to a very reasonable minimum—that they would keep the orthodox Easter, and unite with him in the conversion of the English, which included their acceptance of him as their Archbishop.

The Britons, on their side, had agreed among themselves to surrender their old customs; but the point on which they hesitated was that of putting their Church under Augustine's jurisdiction. There is much to be admired, both in the tolerance of Augustine, and the willingness of the Britons to yield on matters which, though of no real importance, were dear to them.

Augustine had tried to make the decision rest upon a miracle; the Britons made it turn upon a prognostic. Before the learned men who had been summoned from Bangor set out on their journey to the synod, they consulted "a certain holy and discreet man who had led an eremitical life among them." Both in the Celtic and Latin monasteries, it was not an unusual thing that some man of specially ascetic disposition lived the life of a recluse in a separate cell within the monastery. Not long after, we find Cuthbert living such a life at Lindisfarne. So late as the fourteenth century, the young King Richard II., before he went out to meet Wat Tyler's mob, consulted a hermit who was living this recluse life in the Monastery of Westminster.

The oracle gave them a characteristically enigmatical reply: "If Augustine is a man of God," he said, "follow him." "But how shall we know that?" said they. He replied, "Our Lord saith, 'Take My yoke upon you, and learn of Me, for I am meek and lowly of heart.' It is to be believed that he has taken upon him the yoke of Christ, and offers the same to you to take upon you. But if he is stern and haughty, it appears that he is not of God, nor are we to regard his words." They insisted again, "And how shall we learn even this?" "Do you contrive," said the anchorite, "that he may first arrive with his company at the place where the synod is to be held; and if, at your approach, he shall rise up to you, hear him submissively, being assured that he is the servant of Christ; but if he shall despise you, and not rise up to you, whereas you are more in number, let him also be despised by you."

Let it be noted that the real point in question was the acceptance of obedience to the See of Canterbury; and that the British Church was prepared, both to conform without reserve to the customs of the continental Churches, to unite with Augustine in forming one Church, and to accept under his leadership their share in the conversion of the English. What an opportunity lost! While we admire the large-heartedness of the general willingness to surrender cherished customs, and to accept a novel yoke, let us not despise the practical sagacity of the "discreet and holy hermit." The inclination of straws shows which way the wind blows. The very heart of the question was the spirit in which Augustine as a ruler would exercise his authority; and the manner of his reception of them was a fair test of the spirit in which he regarded them now, and would treat them afterwards.

Alas! as they approached the place of meeting, they found Augustine seated in a chair under the shadow of the great oak tree famous in after ages as

Augustine's Oak, surrounded by his attendant priests and monks. The more numerous company which approached him consisted of seven bishops, the monks of Bangor, and others their most learned men, the formal representatives of the ancient and independent British Church. Alas! Augustine retained his seat, like a sovereign receiving a humble deputation of his subjects. The question was decided. They said among themselves, "If he would not now rise up to us, how much more will he condemn us as of no worth, if we shall put ourselves under his subjection?"

The proceedings of the conference which followed are briefly summed up by the historian. Augustine said to them: "You act in many particulars contrary to our custom, or rather the custom of the universal Church; yet if you will comply with me in these three points, viz. to keep Easter at the due time; to administer baptism, by which we are again born to God, according to the custom of the holy Roman Apostolic Church; and, jointly with us, to preach the Word of God to the English nation, we will readily tolerate all the other things you do, though contrary to our customs." They answered, "They would do none of these things, nor receive him as their Archbishop."

There is a very unpleasant sequel to the history of the synod which must not be omitted, since it reflects light upon the beliefs of the time, and introduces an important event in the history of the people. "Augustine is said, in a threatening manner, to have foretold that, if they would not join in unity with their brethren, they should be warred upon by their enemies; and if they would not preach the way of life to the English nation, they should at their hands undergo the vengeance of death."

Very likely Augustine, in the anger of his disappointment, said words to that effect. They were the obvious things for an angry man to say in the circumstances. It was the future event which made men recall his words to mind, and assign to them the character of prophecy. A few years afterwards (613 A.D.), when, as we have already had occasion to say, the Northumbrians made another great movement westward, and conquered Bath, Gloucester, and Cirencester, the Britons made a last stand near Chester, and one of the decisive battles of the English conquest was fought, which resulted in the intrusion of the West Saxon territory between Wales and Cumbria. The Welsh authorities say that four princes of the native race had united their force to resist the aggression, viz. Brocmail, the Prince of Powis; Cadvan, King of Britain; Morgan, King of Demetia; and Bledericus, King of Cornwall. One of the incidents of the battle is thus narrated by Bede:—" A great number of priests and monks had come on the field to pray for the success of their fellow-countrymen in the battle." Most of them were of the neighbouring Monastery of Bangor, in which it is reported there was so great a number of monks, that "the monastery was divided into seven parts, with a ruler over each; and none of these parts contained less than three hundred men, who all lived by the labour of their hands." It is a very interesting side-light upon the organisation of the vast Celtic monasteries.

Many of these, having observed a fast of three days, resolved among others to pray at the aforesaid battle; and Brocmail, the Prince of Powis, had been appointed with his followers to protect them.

Ethelred, King of Northumbria, the leader of the English army, inquired who these men were, and, being told of the purpose of their coming, said: "If they cry to their God against us, then, though they do not bear arms, they fight against us with their prayers," and he commanded the first assault to be made against them. Brocmail, seeing his detached post thus attacked by the whole force of the enemy, withdrew his men, and left the hapless monks to be massacred. About twelve hundred of them were slain, and only about fifty escaped by flight; and their monastery fell into the hands of the enemy. The superstition of the time recalled the words of Augustine, and gave to them the character of a prophecy.

We cannot acquit Gregory of having made a great mistake in the light-hearted way in which, in the first instance, he took upon himself to command the British bishops to be instructed and ruled by Augustine. We have had occasion to note other evidences that Gregory knew little or nothing of the actual condition of the British Church of the time.

Augustine, with his local knowledge, better understood the situation, and approached the British Church with a certain amount of diplomatic skill, but his haughty reception of the British bishops and their companions was a lamentable blunder; and it is to be feared that it was characteristic of his temper, and of his view of the relations which were to exist between himself and them. We have very few personal traits of Augustine all through the history, and this is one of the most important of them; and it cannot but influence our general estimate of his character.

We observe that Augustine did not demand the submission of the British Church to the authority of the Roman See as of divine right, or pass any sort of sentence of excommunication upon the bishops for their refusal to accept his proposal. The pretensions of Rome had not yet grown to such a height.

CHAPTER XIX

THE ENDEAVOUR TO EXTEND THE CHURCH TO THE OTHER ENGLISH KINGDOMS

UPON the failure of the Synod of the Oak, the King and Archbishop turned their attention to the extension of the Church to the other nations of the English by their own resources. Throughout the English conversion, political influence and family relations played a very unusually important part in the extension of the work. It was Queen Bertha's Christianity which induced Ethelbert to give a friendly reception to Augustine's mission, and a favourable ear to his teaching. Now it is Ethelbert's political influence as Bretwalda which makes a way for the extension of the good work to the neighbouring kingdoms. In the year 604, says Bede, Augustine, Archbishop of Britain, ordained two bishops, viz. Mellitus and Justus, to Episcopal Sees at London and at Rochester.

The Saxons who conquered and settled in the part of the country between the Thames and the Stour, and who penetrated for some miles westward of London, probably came under several independent leaders, but for some generations they had been united into one Kingdom of the East Saxons, with a tribal division into East Saxons (Essex) and Middle Saxons (Middlesex), and London was the capital of the kingdom.

London had been a Roman town, not a great fortress, but a considerable emporium of trade. Whether the invaders sacked and burnt it and left it waste, or whether the tide of invasion flowed round it and left it uninjured, no ancient history has recorded, and the modern historians are not agreed upon the subject. But if the former were the case, the site was one which offered commercial advantages so great that it would not long be left unoccupied. In those days, the Thames below London spread over the low lands on each side of its present confined bed, and presented the appearance at high tide of a great arm of the sea, into which the river entered at about the point where London stands; and there a rising ground above the marshes afforded a good site for a town. Moreover, it was the first place where travellers who had landed at Richborough and coasted the south side of this arm of the sea, could conveniently cross to the northern side of the barrier and gain access to the heart of the country. It is probable that there was a bridge here as early as the Roman times. Bede says that at this time it was "the mart of many nations, resorting to it by sea and land." It would therefore be an important position for the establishment of a new centre of missionary work. The late King, Sledda, had sought Ricula, a sister of Ethelbert, in marriage; Seberht was therefore Ethelbert's nephew. Bede says that Ethelbert had placed him upon the throne, which looks as if Ethelbert had made himself master of the East Saxons by force of arms, and had continued Seberht as sub-King, according to the usual policy of the times.

We are told nothing of the details of the conversion, but we seem to gather that Seberht was invited to the court of the Bretwalda, and there, by the influence of Ethelbert and the teaching of Augustine, was induced to embrace the faith, and to consent to countenance the endeavours of Mellitus to convert the East Saxon people. Again, we are not told whether Mellitus went first, according to the usual ecclesiastical policy of the time, and gathered a Christian flock together, and then came back to Canterbury for ordination as a bishop over them; or whether, as in the subsequent case of Paulinus, he was consecrated at once, and returned with King Seberht to begin to gather a flock out of the East Saxon people, under the King's protection and influence. What we are told is that Ethelbert built the first church in London. We know from the subsequent narrative that Mellitus laboured there during the remaining twelve years of Seberht's life and reign, and from the apostasy of the people and the flight of Mellitus on Seberht's death, we gather that his labours were not very successful.

The case of Rochester presents some features difficult to explain. We suppose that, as the East Saxon kingdom was made up out of various independent groups of settlements, which had first coalesced into two groups, the East Saxon and the Middle Saxon, and the chief of the East Saxons had finally combined the two groups into one kingdom, so there had been a subdivision of the Jutes, who had occupied the north-west corner of Kent (perhaps under the leadership of Rholf), and had accepted, or been reduced by arms to submit to, the rule of the King of Kent. We are told, without any details, that Augustine ordained Justus as Bishop at Rochester, and that Ethelbert built him a church there, which was dedicated to St. Andrew (the patron saint, it will be remembered, of Gregory's monastery on the Cælian Hill).

There was always a special relation between the Bishop of Rochester and the Archbishop of Kent, which seems to arise out of the relations between this north-western tribe and the rest of the kingdom. The Bishop of Rochester was the Archbishop's suffragan in a special sense; he was always nominated by the Archbishop, he took a special vow of obedience to the Archbishop, and acted as his cross-bearer.

It was probably about the same time that an attempt was made to introduce Christianity into the Kingdom of East Anglia. In this case we are expressly told that Redwald, the King of the East Angles, was admitted to the sacrament of the Christian faith in Kent. No bishop was consecrated for East Anglia, but Redwald must, from what we are subsequently told, have taken a priest back with him. The attempt, however, did not succeed. We have here another of the numerous examples of the influence of women of high birth in the English conversion, but this time it was exercised effectively against the faith. Redwald, on his return home, found himself opposed by his Queen and "certain perverse teachers," in his wish to introduce Christianity. The result was an unseemly compromise. "In the same temple he had an altar to sacrifice to Christ" for his own worship, "and another small one to offer victims to devils" for the worship of his Queen no doubt, after the national rites to which she adhered. In such circumstances, it is not wonderful that the new faith made no impression on the people; and on Redwald's death entirely died out. To anticipate a little, Eorpwald, the son of Redwald, was converted in Northumbria, under the influence of King Edwin, but was shortly assassinated. Sigebert, the brother and successor of Eorpwald, returned from exile in Burgundy a Christian, and his people were at length Christianised by Felix the Burgundian and Fursey the Celt.

CHAPTER XX

THE EPISCOPACY OF LAURENTIUS

THE consecration of Mellitus and Justus, the establishment of the new mission centres in Rochester and London, are the last recorded incidents of Augustine's work, with the exception of that which was to provide a successor to himself. We have no knowledge of Augustine's age, and cannot tell whether it was a feeling of growing infirmities or a premonition of mortal sickness which led him to provide for the succession in his own lifetime.

When Mellitus and Justus were put at the head of the new missions, and promoted to the dignity of the episcopate, Augustine retained by his own side one who had still higher claims, to be his own assistant and successor. Laurentius the Priest would seem to have been the ablest of the band of men who came to Britain with Augustine. It was he whom Augustine sent back to Rome, to convey the news of the success of the mission, and to ask for further directions. He conducted the second mission party from Rome, through Gaul, to Britain; and in the letters of introduction which the party carried from Gregory to the rulers and bishops of Gaul, " Laurentius the Priest, my dearly beloved son, whose devotion is well known to me," is always mentioned before Mellitus the Abbot, as the head of the party. It was Laurentius whom Augustine had chosen to be his successor. His reason for consecrating him himself, in his own lifetime, instead of leaving his consecration to Mellitus and Justus, with or without the assistance of some of the Gallic bishops, is stated by Bede. It was, "lest, upon his death, the state of the Church, as yet unsettled, might begin to falter, if it should be destitute of a pastor, yea, but an hour." Augustine would probably associate Mellitus and Justus with himself in the consecration. Laurentius was consecrated early in 604; in a charter of Ethelbert, making a grant to Rochester, the genuineness of which is not disputed, Laurentius is described as already bishop, on 28th April 604.

During the remainder of Augustine's life Laurentius would be his coadjutor-bishop; that remainder was not a long one. In the following spring—probably 26th May, 605—the Apostle of Kent died, and went to his reward. The new monastery being not yet so far advanced that the first Archbishop could be at once placed in its north porch, according to the design of its founders, he was temporarily buried in the ground near at hand.

The death of Augustine does not bring our narrative to a natural conclusion. His work continued after his death in the hands of his companions. The time was not come for forming an estimate of the man and the work as a whole. It is the same work, carried on on the same lines, though the main direction of it passes from Augustine to Laurentius, from Laurentius to Mellitus, from Mellitus to Justus, from Justus to Honorius; and the history comes to its natural termination when Theodore of Tarsus comes in from outside and begins a new era.

The episcopate of Laurentius extended over fifteen years. During the earlier portion of it the great work in hand was the building of the new monastery. Ethelbert and Bertha, with their nobles, are said to have celebrated there the Christmas of 605 A.D.

Laurentius "laboured indefatigably, both by frequent exhortations and examples of piety, to raise to perfection the foundations of the Church which had been so nobly laid. Nor did he limit his solicitude to the Kentish men. He, associating with himself his brother bishops, wrote a letter to the Scots of Ireland, which is full of information as to the religious situation. It begins:—

> "To our most dear Brothers the Lord Bishops and Abbots throughout all Scotland[1]— Laurentius, Mellitus, and Justus, Servants of the Servants of God.

"When the Apostolic See, according to the universal custom which it has followed elsewhere,[2] sent us to these western parts to preach to pagan nations, we came into this island which is called Britain, without possessing any previous knowledge of its inhabitants. We held both the Britons and Scots in great esteem for sanctity, believing that they had proceeded according to the custom of the Early Church. On becoming acquainted with the errors of the Britons, we still thought that the Scots had been

---

[1] *I.e.* Ireland. The Scots were the predominant population in Ireland, and that island was generally called *Scotia*, or *Insula Scotorum*, by the writers of the sixth and seventh centuries. The name *Scotia*, or Scotland, as applied to the northern half of Britain, is of comparatively modern origin.

[2] A very bold statement, not borne out by the facts of history.

better; but we have been informed by Bishop Dagan [said to have belonged to Bangor in Ireland], coming into this aforesaid island, and by the Abbot Columbanus in France,[1] that the Scots in no way differ from

[1] This dispute between the two schools about the time of Easter had been introduced into Gaul by the mission of Columbanus. As early as the year 599, a correspondence had taken place between that eminent missionary—the founder of Annegray, Luxeuil, Bregenz, and Bobbio—and Gregory, in which the Celtic Apostle expresses all due reverence for Gregory's position, but asserts his own independence, and refuses to alter what he believes to be right. A little later— 602 A.D.—the Frank bishops convened a synod to consider how they should act towards him. He expresses his thankfulness that he has been the occasion of their meeting in synod, and wishes that they met more frequently, as the canons require. He refers them to his correspondence with Gregory on the Eastern question, and concludes with an eloquent appeal, which is worth extracting, as an illustration of the spirit of the Celtic fathers, even while asserting their independence and adhering to their own customs:—"I came as a stranger among you, on behalf of our common Lord and Master, Jesus Christ. In His name, I beseech you, let me live in peace and quiet, as I have lived for twelve years in these woods, beside the bones of my seventeen departed brethren. Let Gaul receive into her bosom all who, if they deserve it, will meet in one heaven. For we have one kingdom promised us, and one hope of our calling in Christ, with whom we shall reign together, if first we suffer with Him here on earth. Choose ye which rule respecting Easter ye prefer to follow, remembering the words of the apostle: '*Prove all things; hold fast that which is good.*' But let us not quarrel one with another, lest our enemies, the Jews, the heretics, and pagan Gentiles, rejoice in our contention." And he concludes: "Pray for us, my fathers, even as we, humble as we are, pray for you. Regard us not as strangers, for we are members together of one body, whether we be Gauls, or Britons, or Iberians, or to whatever nation we belong. Therefore let us all rejoice in the knowledge of the faith and the revelation of the Son of God, and let us strive earnestly to attain together, even to the perfect man, to the measure of the stature of the fulness of Christ, in communion with whom let us learn to love one another, and praise one another, and correct one another, and pray for one another, that with Him we may together reign for evermore."

the Britons in their behaviour; for Bishop Dagan coming to us not only refused to eat with us, but even to take his repast in the same house where we were entertained." The English bishops also wrote a letter to the priests of Britain, in which they repeated the old exhortations to Catholic unity, but with no success.

About this time, says Bede, Mellitus, Bishop of London, went to Rome, to confer with Pope Boniface, Gregory's successor, about the necessary affairs of the English Church. He gives us no clue to the nature of the affairs, and the importance of the note lies in the knowledge it conveys, that communication was maintained with Rome, of which we shall have several subsequent instances.

While Mellitus was at Rome, a synod of Italian bishops was held, which Mellitus attended, " that also by his authority he might confirm such things as should be regularly decreed, and at his return into Britain, might carry the same to the churches of the English to be prescribed and observed."

The Abbey Church of SS. Peter and Paul was at length completed and ready to be consecrated in the time of Laurentius, but in what year is not known; Thorn gives it as 613. The remains of Augustine were then taken from their temporary resting-place in the ground hard by, and deposited in the north *porticus*; and the name of St. Augustine was associated with those of SS. Peter and Paul in the dedication.

CHAPTER XXI

THE DEATH OF ETHELBERT; THE APOSTASY

THE greatest event in the episcopate of Laurentius was the death of Ethelbert, which took place 24th February, 616 A.D. He was buried in the south portico of the newly-consecrated Church of St. Augustine's Abbey, which had been always intended to be the royal mausoleum.

The results which followed upon his death shed back light upon the character of the man, and open up a new revelation of the present religious condition of the people. Ethelbert was peacefully succeeded by his son Eadbald. The fact that the Bretwaldaship at once passed away from Kent to Redwald, King of the East Angles, who had been subservient to Ethelbert, not as the result of any victory of East Anglia over Kent, seems to lead to the inference that it was the different character of Ethelbert and Eadbald which led to the changed political relations between the Kingdom of Kent and the other southern kingdoms.

Now, too, we learn how much the work of the Church among the English had been indebted to the authority and influence of Ethelbert; for on his death occurred a great and widespread reaction which threatened the work of Augustine with destruction. We are a little surprised to find that Eadbald had never been baptized, and as soon as he was his own master he revolted from the restraint of Christianity. He was urged thereto by the desire to contract a marriage in a forbidden degree, about which Augustine long ago had consulted Gregory, as if he had found it a common custom among the heathen Kentish men, for on his father's death he took his widowed stepmother in marriage. We thus, for the first time, become acquainted with the fact that Queen Bertha had been sometime dead, and that Ethelbert had married again. Who the new Queen was is quite unknown, the historians appear to have purposely withheld all information about her. The King's example led others who had abandoned unlawful connections to revert to them, and encouraged all who were disinclined to the new religion.

Shortly after, Seberht, King of the East Saxons, died, leaving his three sons as his heirs. They had seemed to conform to Christianity during their father's lifetime, but now they reverted to the old religion, and granted liberty to all their people to follow their evil example. An anecdote which Bede relates proves that these three East Saxon princes had not been baptized; and we are led to the serious inference that if the very sons of the Christian kings were still outside the pale of the Church, it is most likely that many others of their principal men, and great numbers of the common people, were still heathen. The East Saxon princes compelled Mellitus and his followers to depart from their kingdom.

The details of the reaction at Rochester are not recorded. All we know is that Justus abandoned his See, and both Mellitus and Justus retired to

Canterbury. On consultation, "it was unanimously agreed that it was better for them all to return to their own country, where they might serve God in freedom, than to continue without any advantage among those barbarians who had revolted from the faith." The words seem to mean that the apostasy was very general, and that the whole body of the Italians proposed to abandon the work. "Mellitus and Justus accordingly went first, and withdrew into France, designing there to await the event of things. . . Laurentius, being about to follow them, and to quit Britain," ordered his bed to be laid on the last night in the church of the monastery. There, Bede relates, St. Peter appeared to him, scourged him severely, and demanded "why he would forsake the flock which he had committed to him? or to what shepherds would he commit Christ's sheep that were in the midst of wolves?" and other words to the same purpose. We might explain this as the vivid dream of a mind harassed and excited by doubts of the lawfulness of abandoning the work, but that the sequel of the narrative asserts that the stripes were real. What can be said about the supernatural scourging? Is it possible that St. Peter's reproaches, in his dream, awakened his conscience to the sin of deserting the post of duty, and that, in his dream, St. Peter enjoined the penance which the bishop therefore attributes to the apostle, though the stripes were inflicted by his own hand? Next morning Laurentius went to the King, stripped his shoulders, and showed him the marks of the stripes which he had received. The King asked in astonishment who had dared thus to ill-treat so great a man; whereupon Laurentius told his vision. The preternatural occurrence had so great an effect upon Eadbald, that he abjured the worship of idols, renounced his unlawful marriage, embraced the faith of Christ, was baptized, and promoted the welfare of the Church to the utmost of his power. The nameless Queen ultimately appears to have retired with a daughter, Mildred, to the Monastery of Lyminge. Eadbald soon after sought for a wife, after his father's example, in the house of Clovis, and married Emma, the daughter of Theodebert, King of Austrasia.

The East Saxon princes were shortly afterwards slain in battle against the West Saxons; but the people "having turned back to their old idolatry, would not be corrected nor return to the unity of faith and charity which is in Christ." For when Eadbald sent over to France and recalled Mellitus and Justus, just a year after their departure, Justus had no difficulty in resuming his See at Rochester; but the Londoners would not receive their bishop back again, choosing rather to be under their idolatrous high-priest. It does not appear that any progress had been made among the East Saxons outside London. The evangelisation of the whole people had to wait till Cedd came from Lindisfarne and set up mission stations at Ithanacester (Bradwell-on-Sea) on the Blackwater, and at East Tilbury on the Thames; his successor Earconwald set up his bishop-stool again in London.

CHAPTER XXII

THE MISSION TO NORTHUMBRIA

IT is probable that Bishop Laurentius died soon after the events last mentioned, in the year 619 A.D. He was succeeded in the See of Canterbury by Mellitus, who appears to have been living there since his final expulsion from London. He ruled the Church of Canterbury for five years. We know little about him. He was noble by birth, but much nobler in mind, " cheerfully passing over all earthly things, and always aspiring to love, seek, and attain to those which are celestial." It gives a touch of human interest to know that he was subject to gout. On one occasion, when an accidental fire was raging among the timber buildings of the city, and a south wind was carrying the conflagration towards the cathedral buildings, the bishop had himself carried to the flames, and a change in the direction of the wind from south to north, which stopped the progress of the flames, was attributed to his prayers. The incidental statement that the Church of the Four Crowned Martyrs stood at the place where the fire raged most, acquaints us with the fact that another church, with that dedication, had been built in the city, probably to afford accommodation to the increasing number of Christians among its population. The unusual dedication of this new church is accounted for in an interesting way. Honorius, Bishop of Rome, built a church in 626 A.D. to the Four Crowned Martyrs (Carporferus, Severus, Severianus, and Victorianus), on the ridge of the Cælian Hill. As the Roman missionaries had dedicated Rochester Cathedral to St. Andrew, the patron saint of their old monastery, and the temple on whose site the monastery was built to St. Pancras, because their old monastery was partly on the site of the estates of the family of the boy martyr, so now they give to their new church the same dedication as that of Honorius's church in the near neighbourhood of their old home at Rome. Ethelbald built a church, dedicated to the Blessed Virgin Mary, eastward of the great Church of St. Augustine's monastery, which was consecrated by Mellitus. Mellitus died in 624 A.D., and was buried with his predecessors in the north *porticus* of the monastic church.

Justus, Bishop of Rochester, succeeded Mellitus in the archbishopric, and consecrated Romanus as Bishop of Rochester in his own stead. He seems to have thought it necessary to obtain the sanction of the Bishop of Rome for this step. Boniface sent him the pall, which neither of his two latest predecessors had received, together with a verbose letter, of which it is only necessary to give one sentence. "We have also, brother, encouraged by zeal for what is good, sent you, by the bearer of these, the pall, which we have only given leave to use in the celebration of the sacred mysteries; granting you likewise to ordain bishops when there shall be occasion, through the mercy of our Lord; that so the gospel of Christ, by the preaching of many, may be spread abroad in all the nations that are not yet converted."

Justus occupied the See for three years. In his time occurred the most interesting episode in the whole history of the mission, the extension of Christianity to Northumbria. When the scene of the history is transformed to Northumbria, Bede's narrative at once becomes more full and picturesque, and we recognise that, while Bede was dependent for summaries of the annals of Kent upon his correspondent Abbot Nothelm, he is on his own ground in Northumbria, and selects at his own discretion, and with considerable literary skill, from the abundance of material within his reach.

Again a royal marriage opened the way for the pioneers of the Church. Edwin, King of Northumbria, sent ambassadors to Eadbald of Kent to ask for his sister Ethelburga in marriage. Here our history repeats itself. Eadbald replied that it was not lawful to marry a Christian maiden to a pagan husband, lest the faith and the mysteries of the Heavenly King should be profaned by her union with a king who was altogether a stranger to the worship of the true God. Edwin replied, that he would in no way act against the Christian faith, that he would allow his wife and all who accompanied her, men or women, priests or ministers, to follow their faith and worship after the Christian customs; and that he would not refuse to embrace that religion himself, if, being examined by wise persons, it should be found more holy and more worthy of God. Upon these conditions the alliance of the northern King was accepted. The surviving Italians of the first mission company must have lifted up their hearts with hopeful joy when they heard that at last, after so many disappointments with the British Church, the abortive attempt in East Anglia, the failure in London, a way was opened to that very Deira which had been their goal when they first started from their monastery on the Cælian Hill; and their interest and prayers would add to the enthusiasm with which Paulinus set out on his journey.

It is evident, from a collation of various passages which bear upon the subject, that in this rude English society, as in later times, a Queen had a household of her own, and that the Kentish princess went to the court of Northumbria with a number of attendants, men and women. It also appears probable, from several passages, that a royal Christian bride was accompanied by a chaplain of her own countrymen, to be her adviser and the ruler of her household, even when the marriage was between Christians, much more was this desirable in such a case as the present.

Paulinus, one of the men who came into Kent with Mellitus, was chosen to be the princess's chaplain, accompanied probably by James the Deacon; and as the chaplain who came from France with Bertha was a bishop, so to do honour to Ethelburga, and to give her chaplain the greater authority, Justus consecrated Paulinus as a bishop on the 21st July, 625 A.D. The bride, with her attendants and a gallant escort, probably embarked at Richborough, and went northward by sea, disembarking at Bamborough, where they would be met by Edwin and his thanes and knights, and so they were married by Paulinus with great solemnity.

Here again we have an evidence that occasional communication was maintained between Canterbury and Rome, and that the successors of Gregory took an interest in this Roman mission. For Boniface, hearing of this hopeful event, endeavoured to improve it by the prestige of his office, and the power of his persuasion. As Gregory had written to Ethelbert and Bertha, so now Boniface wrote to Edwin and Ethelburga.

The letter is long and verbose, so that it may be better to give only a summary of its contents. It began by saying "that the greatness of God, existing in invisible and unsearchable eternity, cannot be comprehended or expressed by human wit; but He has been pleased to inspire into the minds of men such things concerning Himself as He was willing to make known to them; and he (the Bishop) has thought fit to extend his priestly care to the King, and to make known to him the Christian faith, which our Saviour Christ commanded should be preached to all nations, in order to offer to him the cup of life and salvation.

"Thus the goodness of the Supreme Majesty by the word of His command created all things, the heavens, the earth, the sea, and all that is in them, disposing the order in which they should subsist; and with the counsel of His co-eternal Word and the unity of the Holy Spirit, He formed man out of the slime of the earth, and gave him such supereminent prerogative as to place him above all others; so that, observing the commands given to him, His continuance should be to all eternity. . . . How great guilt, then, they lie under who adhere to the pernicious superstitions of the worship of idols, appears by the perdition of those whom they worship; wherefore it is said of them in the Psalms, 'All the gods of the Gentiles are devils, but the Lord made the heavens.' And again, 'They have eyes and see not,' etc.

"It behoves you, therefore, to take upon you the sign of the Holy Cross, by which the human race is redeemed, and to break in pieces those idols which you have worshipped; for the very destruction of them, which could never receive life or sense from their makers, may plainly demonstrate how worthless they were, since you yourselves who have received life from the Lord are certainly better than they. Draw near, then, to the knowledge of Him who made you, who breathed the breath of life into you, who sent His only-begotten Son for your redemption, to cleanse you from original sin, that, being delivered from the power of the devil's wickedness, He might bestow on you a heavenly reward.

"Hear the words of the preachers, and the gospel of God which they declare to you, to the end that believing in God the Father Almighty, and in Jesus Christ His Son, and in the Holy Spirit, the indivisible Trinity, and being born again by water and the Holy Ghost, you may, through His assistance and goodness, dwell in the brightness of the eternal glory with Him in whom you shall believe."

It is an interesting sketch of a missionary sermon. The Bishop concludes by sending the blessing of St. Peter, and sundry presents—a tunic, a gold ornament, and a garment of Ancyra, which he prays his Highness to accept with the same friendship with which they are sent.

At the same time, the Bishop sent a letter to

Ethelburga, which also we shall take leave to summarise. He says that his mind has been much rejoiced that the Lord has vouchsafed, in her Highness' conversion, to kindle a spark of the orthodox religion, by which the more easily to inflame the mind, not only of her glorious consort, but also of the nation that is subject to them.

For he has been informed by messengers who were sent to him, of the laudable conversion of his illustrious son, King Eadbald, and that she likewise was so wholly taken up with the love of her Redeemer, that she never ceased to lend her assistance for the propagation of the Christian faith. But it had caused him no small grief to learn that her illustrious husband still served abominable idols, and would not yield obedience or give ear to the preachers. Wherefore he exhorts her, to the utmost of her power, to endeavour to soften the hardness of his heart, and to inflame his coldness, that the Scripture may be fulfilled by her, and "the unbelieving husband be saved by the believing wife"; and assures her that he does not cease, with frequent prayers, to beg that she may be able to perform this.

He concludes by sending her the blessing of St. Peter, and a present consisting of a silver looking-glass and a gilt ivory comb.[1]

[1] Boniface v. died, Oct., 625 A.D., so that these letters were written before that date.

CHAPTER XXIII

Progress of the Work in Northumbria

It will be well to pause here, in order to consider the condition of this new district to which we are introduced. The settlements of the Angles from the Humber, northwards, were among the earliest, but they seem at first to have been only along the coast. The invaders forced their way inland slowly, against tenacious resistance, and with varying fortunes; for they had not only to fight against the Britons and drive them westward, but they had to guard their right flank, which, the further they extended their conquests, was the more and more exposed to attack from the Picts and Scots. Cumbria was still independent, and continued to be ruled by native kings till the early part of the tenth century. It would be difficult to define the boundary between the two countries at this time. Long after the period at which we have arrived, there were two small independent British districts, Loidis and Elmet, in the West Riding of Yorkshire. The town of Leeds takes its name from the former, and the village of Barwick-in-Elmet defines the whereabouts of the latter. The war of conquest, which had ceased a century ago in Kent and the south-east of the island generally, was still of doubtful issue in the north; not many years after the very period at which we have arrived, a confederation of the Britons under Cædwalla, aided by Penda, King of Mercia, recovered the whole country, as we shall presently see.

As for the religious condition of the north, the Britons of Cumbria were the descendants of the Church of the old Roman province; and the disciples of Ninian, of Kentigern, and of Columba, were scattered among the Picts and Scots. Nennius asserts that a Welshman, Rhun, son of Urien, converted the Northumbrians; the *Welsh Chronicle* gives the year 626 A.D. as the date of his labours; and this may be the distorted record of some missionary enterprise immediately preceding the time of the appearance of Paulinus on the scene.[1]

The history of Edwin is briefly this. The Northumbrians had been divided into two kingdoms, Bernicia and Deira, governed by two branches of the house of Ida the Conqueror. On the death of Ælle of Deira— the Ælle of the story of Gregory and the English slaves in the Forum—Æthelfrith, King of Bernicia, made himself master of Deira also, and Ælle's son Edwin, a child of three years old, and his friends, sought refuge in other lands. Edwin wandered from kingdom to kingdom, till he found a refuge at the court of Redwald, King of the East Angles. Æthelfrith sent messengers offering a large sum for the life of the fugitive, and again with a larger bribe, and still again with threats of war.

Redwald was disposed to surrender the fugitive rather than risk the hazard of war. A trusty friend of Edwin warned him of the danger, advised him to

[1] Professor Ray's *Celtic Britain*, p. 130.

flee, and offered to be his guide to a place of safety. The friend may very probably have been sent by Redwald, who hoped thus to evade his difficulty; but Edwin refused. "I thank you for your good will," he said, "but I cannot do what you propose, or be guilty of breaking the compact I have made with so great a King, when he has done me no harm nor offered me any injury. If I must die, let it be by his hand rather than by that of any meaner person. For whither shall I now flee, when I have for so many years been a wanderer through all the provinces of Britain to escape the hands of my enemies?"

While Edwin sat outside the palace, in the dark, brooding over his condition, a stranger appeared to him, who asked what reward he would give to the man who should persuade Redwald not to deliver him up to his enemies. Edwin replied that he would give him all he was able to give. "But what if I also promise that you shall overcome your enemies, and surpass in power all who have reigned before you over the English nation?" Edwin promised that he would make a suitable return to him who should accomplish this. "But," persisted the stranger, "if he can also give you better advice for your life and salvation than any of your progenitors ever heard of, will you consent to submit to him and to follow his wholesome counsel?" Edwin promised that he would in all things follow the counsel of the man who should deliver him from his calamities and raise him to a throne. The stranger then laid his hand upon Edwin's head, saying, "When this sign shall be given you, remember this discourse, and fulfil your promises"; and the stranger disappeared.

While Edwin still sat musing on this which had happened, his friend came again to announce that he might enter the palace and sleep without fear, for Redwald had listened to the expostulations of his Queen, that it was unworthy of so great a King to sell his friend in distress for gold, and to sacrifice his honour, which is more valuable than all other ornaments, for money.

So, dismissing Æthelfrith's messengers, Redwald anticipated his anger; for he gathered his forces, marched against Æthelfrith before he had time to complete his hostile preparations, defeated and slew him, and placed Edwin upon the Northumbrian throne.

Paulinus was diligent, not only in ministration to the little flock of Kentish Christians who formed the Queen's household, but also in endeavours to win some of the pagans to the faith; in his pastoral duty with satisfactory results, but in his missionary efforts with no success. Next year an assassin, sent by Cwichelm, King of the West Saxons, made an attempt upon the life of Edwin. Lilla, the King's minister, who was present, having no buckler at hand to ward off the blow, interposed his own body to receive the stroke, and died for his lord. The same night, which was Easter Sunday, the Queen brought forth a daughter, and the King gave thanks to his gods for her birth. Paulinus, who was present, endeavoured to persuade him that it was to Christ he ought to return his thanks, both for his own escape from death, and for the gift of his child. The King, in the exalted feeling of the moment, promised that, if God would give him life and victory over the King who had so basely sought to slay him, he would cast off his idols and serve Christ; and as a pledge of his promise he gave up his daughter to Paulinus to be consecrated to Christ. And on the following Whitsunday the child was baptized by the name of Eanflæda, with twelve others of her family, who had been won by the teaching of Paulinus, the first-fruits to Christ of the Northumbrian nation.

The King fought a campaign against the West Saxons, to avenge Cwichelm's treacherous attempt against his life, and returned victorious. But though he abandoned the worship of idols, "he would not immediately and unadvisedly embrace the mysteries of the Christian faith, but thought fit first, at leisure, to be instructed by the venerable Paulinus in the knowledge of the faith, and to confer with such as he knew to be the wisest of his chief men; and, being a man of extraordinary sagacity, he often sat alone by himself a long time, silent, but deliberating in his heart how he should proceed, and which religion he should adhere to." One day, while he sat thus meditating, Paulinus came to him, and, laying his right hand upon his head, asked whether he remembered that sign. The King was ready to fall at his feet, but Paulinus raised him up, and said, "Behold, by the help of God you have escaped from the hands of the enemies whom you feared, you have obtained the kingdom which you desired; do not delay to fulfil the promise you made." The King declared that he was willing to receive the faith, but would confer with his principal friends and chief advisers about it, that, if they were of his opinion, they might together be cleansed in the fountain of Christ. So the King submitted to his Witan the question whether they should embrace the religion of Christ.

The consultation of the Witan, revealing in several typical speeches the various motives which influenced the minds of these Englishmen, in abandoning the old religion and embracing the new, is one of the most interesting passages in our Church history. Coifi, the chief priest, was the first to speak: "O King, take this new doctrine into consideration; for I declare to you most truly what I have learned for certain, that the religion which we have hitherto professed has no power or goodness in it. For none of your people has applied himself more diligently to the worship of our gods than I; and yet there are many who receive greater favours from you, and are more preferred than I, and are more prosperous in their undertakings. Now, if the gods availed anything, they would rather forward me, who have been more careful to serve them. It remains, therefore, that if, upon examination, you find these new doctrines better and more efficacious, we immediately receive them without any delay."

These were the worldly old high priest's views of religion; and they no doubt represent one phase of false religion, which worships the gods in the hope of worldly advantage, and is ready to declare them good for nothing if they do not give it. It is a very human view, and exists among Christians also. But there is a nobler phase of mind among heathens as among Christians, and the next speech represents it—a yearning after the solution of the awful mystery of life.

Another of the King's chief men said: "The present

life of man, O King, compared with the time which is unknown to us, seems to me like the swift flight of a sparrow through the hall wherein you sit in winter with your commanders and ministers, and a good fire in the midst, while storms of rain and snow prevail outside; the sparrow, I say, flies swiftly through the house, in at one door and immediately out at the other. Whilst he is in he is safe from the wintry storm, but after a short space of fair weather he immediately vanishes out of your sight into the dark winter from which he came. So this life of man appears for a short space; but of what went before or what is to follow we are utterly ignorant. If this new doctrine teaches something more certain, it seems justly to deserve to be followed."

Other elders and counsellors spoke to the same effect. Paulinus was then invited to address the assembly. Bede has not given the least hint of the tenor of his speech. We may refer to Boniface's letter to the King for the kind of general argument which Paulinus with his local knowledge would apply to the particular occasion; and Coifi's echo of it is "truth, life, salvation, eternal happiness." For the high priest had been lifted to a higher level of thought by Paulinus's discourse, and he replied to it: "I have long known that there was nothing in that which we worshipped, for the more diligently I sought after truth in that worship the less I found it. But I freely confess that such truth evidently appears in this preaching as can confer on us the gifts of life, salvation, and eternal happiness. Therefore I advise, O King, that we abjure that worship, and set fire to those temples and altars from which we have derived no benefit." Coifi volunteered to take the first step in this resolution. Mounting the King's horse and bearing arms, both unlawful to the priest, he galloped to the neighbouring temple of Godmundingaham, and desecrated it by casting his spear into it, in the presence of a multitude of people, and then commanded the temple and its enclosures to be destroyed by fire. The place was not far from York. It appears that the temple and its enclosures were of timber.

The King and all the nobles of the nation, and a large number of the commons, received the faith. While waiting for Easter, they were catechised and instructed. A timber church was erected over a spring in the city of York, and herein, on the Easter Sunday, 627 A.D., Edwin was baptized, and we assume that his thanes and knights and many of the common people were baptized at the same time. Edwin appointed York, the principal town of Deira, as the See of Paulinus, and began to build a basilican church of stone around the wooden oratory. This church of stone grew slowly—it was not finished till the time of Oswald, his successor; but it has virtually lasted till now, for the present York Minster occupies the same site, embodies the stones of Edwin's and Oswald's church, and the spring from which Edwin was baptized still exists in the crypt. We search with natural interest for any indication of the character of the building. Bede says that it was built under Paulinus's instructions (*docente eodem Paulino*), therefore we should expect it to be of the basilican type then usual; but he says that it was square (*per quadrum cœpit edificare basilicam*)—does that mean that it had not the usual semicircular apse? The royal children were buried in the church, and afterwards we learn that Edwin was buried in the *porticus* of St. Gregory. Did Paulinus adopt the plan of Augustine's Church of St. Peter and St. Paul at Canterbury, and add a *porticus* for the royal mausoleum? A square-ended church, with lateral porches or transepts, would be an approach to the common plan of later times. Fragments of this Saxon church have been discovered in the course of modern repairs. The well is circular, and the high altar always stood immediately over it until the changes made in 1736 A.D.

Then, or soon after, the members of the royal family were baptized—two sons, Osfrith and Eadfrith, born to him while he was in banishment, by Quenberga, daughter of Cearl, King of the Mercians; and Iffi, son of Osfrith; and of his children by Ethelburga, Ethelhun and his daughter Etheldrith, and another Wuscfrea; besides Eanflæda already mentioned. Ethelhun and his daughter Etheldrith were snatched out of this life whilst still in their white baptismal garments—which it was the custom in the Early Church to wear for eight days after baptism—and were buried in the church at York.

The position of Paulinus in Northumbria was not like that of Augustine in Kent; it was rather like that of Liudhard at the court of Ethelbert. Augustine came with a large staff to preach the gospel to a nation; Paulinus, like Liudhard, was simply the chaplain of the Queen, his chief duty was to minister to her and her Christian attendants, lest in the midst of a heathen court and kingdom they should deteriorate in Christian faith or practice. Even after the conversion of the King and his principal men, and a multitude of the common people, there is no trace of any helpers being sent to him from Kent; and it would be long before any of his English converts were fit to be ordained to the ministry; so that Paulinus and his Deacon were still the only missionaries in Northumbria, and their duty was always with the court.

But Paulinus was of a zealous missionary spirit, and he found opportunities for doing a considerable and successful mission work. A little consideration of Bede's narrative shows that Edwin and Ethelburga, with their numerous court, were accustomed to go to various royal seats, and to make some considerable stay at each place. Had Paulinus been free to plan his missionary work as he pleased, it may be doubted whether he could have laid any wiser plan than that to which his duties limited him. Wherever the court took up its residence for a while, there would be a resort to it of all the influential people of the neighbourhood; and Paulinus would have the opportunity of preaching to them under the present and powerful countenance of the King and Queen.

Paulinus zealously took advantage of these opportunities, and Bede records an instance of the success which attended his labours. "At a certain time, coming with the King and Queen to the royal country-seat which is called Adgefrin, [*i.e.* Yeverin-in-Glendale, near Wooler, in Northumberland,] he stayed there with them thirty-six days, fully occupied in catechising and baptizing, during which days, from morning till night, he did nothing else but instruct the people, resorting thither from all villages and places, in Christ's saving word; and, when instructed, he washed them with the water of absolution in the river Glen [now

Bowent] which is close by." This was in Bernicia; but in Deira also, at the village of Cataract, where he was wont often to be with the King, he pursued the same course, and baptized his converts in the river Swale which runs by the village, "for as yet oratories or baptisteries could not be made in the early infancy of the Church in those parts." Also at Campodunum (probably Doncaster) he built a church, which was burnt, together with all the town, by Cædwalla; but the altar, being of stone, escaped; so we conclude that the church was of timber.

The work of this zealous missionary extended even south of the Humber. The Lindiswaras, who had settled in this district, were not sufficiently strong to maintain their independence in the face of their powerful neighbours, and they were a bone of contention between Northumbria and Mercia. It would seem that the powerful King of Northumbria had lately annexed the province; and it was no doubt on a lengthened visit to it, accompanied by the Queen and Paulinus, that Paulinus embraced the opportunity to try to establish the faith there.

It would seem that Edwin made some considerable stay at Lincoln; for Paulinus not only converted the governor of the town, whose name was Blecca, and all his family, but he built in that city a stone church of beautiful workmanship, which is, perhaps, represented by the modern Church of St. Paul; St. Paul being a contraction, perhaps, of the name of Paulinus.

In the old Roman times Lindum Colonia was the principal city of this part of the country, and its special advantages of situation would make it still the chief town of Lindsey, for it was at the highest navigable point of the river Witham, where the great northern Roman road crossed the river, and the old Roman walls—of which some portions still remain, with the northern gateway—made Lincoln a strong fortress.

A great event took place here, which incidentally gives a date to the residence of the Northumbrian court. Justus, Bishop of Canterbury, departed to Christ in the year 627 A.D., and Honorius was chosen as his successor. Now, Gregory, in sketching his plan for the ecclesiastical organisation of England, had contemplated two Metropolitans, one at London and the other at York, each with his twelve suffragan bishops; and had directed that, when either Metropolitan See was vacated by death, the surviving Metropolitan should consecrate the successor to the vacancy. Acting upon this direction of the sainted founder of the mission, Honorius sought consecration from Paulinus. Learning that he was for the present residing at Lincoln, he came there, glad, no doubt, to be saved the longer journey to Northumbria; and was there consecrated in the year 628 A.D., perhaps in the newly-built stone church of beautiful workmanship. Paulinus, consecrated alone, for the See of Rochester was at that moment vacant by the death of Romanus.

Still another place south of the Humber was the scene of a successful work by the zealous Paulinus. This was the city which, in the English tongue, is called Tiovulfingacester, near the river Trent. Bede tells the story with interesting details. "A certain abbot and priest of the Monastery of Peartaneu [Partney, a cell of Bardeney Abbey, of which Deda was the first abbot], a man of singular veracity, whose name was

Deda, told him that one of the oldest inhabitants had informed him, in relation to the faith of this province, that he himself, with a great number of people, had been baptized in the Trent at noonday by Bishop Paulinus, in the presence of King Edwin. The old man was wont to describe the personal appearance of Paulinus; that he was tall, a little stooping, his hair black, his visage meagre, his nose slender and aquiline, his aspect both venerable and majestic." It is a lifelike portrait, and enables us to picture to ourselves the man who is perhaps the most interesting of the whole number of the Italian missionaries. The city of Tiovulfingacester was probably Southwell, where we conjecture that Edwin was making some stay. Throughout the Middle Ages the Church of Southwell was a peculiar of the Archbishop of York, who had a residence there, and all the parish churches of the county of Nottingham regarded it as their mother church; the people came up to it in procession once a year, and the priests received the blessed oils from it for use in their ministrations. It is a probable conjecture that this dependence of Southwell upon York began with some grant by Edwin to Paulinus at this time.

It has been convenient to delay to this place an episode which belongs to a rather earlier period. There is a various reading in some of the MSS. of Bede's History, which makes Edwin, when pressed to fulfil his promise to adopt the Christian faith, plead for time to consult friendly princes (*amicis principibus*), as well as his chief counsellors, in the hope that they might together accept baptism; and this reading is countenanced by the fact that Edwin did, about that time, induce Eorpwald, King of the East Angles, the son of Redwald, to embrace the faith with his whole province, and to receive the sacraments of Christ. We may reasonably conjecture that Edwin's friendship with the friend of his exile, and his present influence as Bretwalda, had brought Eorpwald to the court of Edwin, just as Redwald his father had visited the court of Ethelbert, and had been won to embrace the faith. On this occasion, though the whole province consented to embrace the faith, the impression was not permanent, for, not long after, Eorpwald was slain and the province relapsed.

Edwin was thirty years of age when the defeat of Æthelfrith placed him upon the throne of united Northumbria; he had reigned eleven years before his conversion, and his reign continued for six years after that event. He was more powerful than all the English kings; he added Anglesea and the Isle of Man to his own dominions by conquest; he compelled the British princes[1] to acknowledge his supremacy, and was recognised as Bretwalda by all the English nations except Kent. It was especially in the later years of his reign that his power was increased, and Bede considers it to have been a reward for his receiving the faith. The power and justice of his rule is expressed in the proverbial saying, that a woman with her new-born babe might walk throughout the island, from sea to sea, without receiving any harm. The beneficence of his rule is illustrated by the story that the King took such care for the good of his nation, that, in several places where he had observed clear springs by the highways, he caused stakes to be

[1] Bede, *Eccl. Hist.* ii. 9 and 20.

fixed, with brass bowls hanging from them, for the convenience of travellers; and no man durst touch them, except for the purpose for which they were intended.

His royal state, unusual in the simple manners of the English, has already been described; his banners were not only borne before him in battle, but also in time of peace; when he rode about his cities, towns, or provinces with his officers, the standard-bearer was wont to go before him; and even when he walked along the streets, that sort of banner which the Romans call Tufa and the English Tuuf—a spear ornamented with a tuft of feathers—was borne before him. It was probably some survival of the state affected by the principal officials of the Roman régime, and a sign of his dignity as Bretwalda.

But we are come to the last scene of his interesting life and reign. Cædwalla, the King of Cumbria, the last great hero of the British race, induced the other independent British princes to join their forces with his, in a great attempt to defeat Edwin and recover the north of England from the invaders. Penda, the fierce and warlike King of the Mercians, influenced probably by jealousy of Edwin's growing power, entered into an unnatural alliance with the Britons. At a great battle, fought on the 12th October, 633 A.D., on the plain of Hæthfield (Hatfield Chase, about seven miles north-east of Doncaster), the Northumbrians were defeated with great slaughter; Edwin and his son Osfrith were slain on the field, and another son, Eadfrith, fell into the hands of Penda. Cædwalla and his Britons overran Northumbria, sparing neither age nor sex, and resolving to cut off all the English race within the borders of Britain. The head of King Edwin was brought to York, and eventually buried in the *porticus* of St. Gregory, of the church which he had founded there.

There seemed no safety for the family of Edwin except in flight. Paulinus did not forget that Queen Ethelburga was his especial charge. The Queen, with Eanflæda the daughter, and Wuscfrea the son of Edwin, and Yffi the son of the slain Osfrith, with their attendants, accompanied by Paulinus, and escorted by Bassus, one of Edwin's knights, fled to the coast, and thence took ship for Kent. They took such portable valuables as they could carry with them, and it is to Paulinus that we must probably attribute the carrying off of a large gold cross and a golden chalice, which were long after shown among the treasures of the Church of Canterbury. James the Deacon was left behind to do what he could for the scattered and persecuted remnant of the Church.

CHAPTER XXIV

Episcopate of Honorius

AND so our history, in 633 A.D., returns again to Canterbury, and we have, after an absence of eight years, to look round and note what changes have taken place while we have been pursuing the episode of the mission to Northumbria.

We have already seen that Bishop Justus died in 627 A.D., and that, with a delay of eighteen months, Honorius, the boy-pupil of Gregory, was consecrated by Paulinus at Lincoln, and now occupied the See of Canterbury. The See of Rochester was vacant; Romanus, its bishop, having been sent by Justus to Rome on some business, of the nature of which we are not told, had been drowned in "the Italian Sea," *i.e.* probably in the Mediterranean in his voyage from Marseilles. At the request of Bishop Honorius and King Eadbald, Paulinus undertook the vacant charge, and continued in it till his death twenty years after.

A rather pathetic incident finds its place of record here. It illustrates the occasional intercourse between Kent and Rome, and the slowness of the correspondence between them. Boniface V. had been succeeded in the Roman See by Honorius I. (625 A.D.). News had come to Rome from Britain of the consecration and mission of Paulinus to Northumbria; of the conversion of King Edwin; and of the other successes of Paulinus, which have been related in the preceding narrative; and of the death of Justus and the succession of Honorius to the See of Canterbury. Honorius of Rome sent back a letter (dated 11th of June, 634 A.D.) of congratulation and exhortation to Edwin, whose body lay on the battlefield at Hatfield, and his head in the *porticus* of St. Gregory at York. He also sent a pall to Paulinus as Archbishop of York, which found Paulinus a fugitive in Kent, with his northern church in ruins. Whether Paulinus wore it as Bishop of Rochester we are not told, but on his death he bequeathed it to his cathedral. Honorius wrote also to his beloved brother of Canterbury, a letter of congratulation and encouragement.

What specially needs notice in these letters, is that the Bishop of Rome says that it was at the request of the two kings Eadbald and Edwin that he had sent palls to Honorius and Paulinus, in the name of St. Peter the Apostle, granting them authority that when the divine grace shall call either of them to Himself, the survivor shall ordain a bishop in the room of him that is deceased. This is merely a repetition of the original arrangement of Gregory, which we have seen Honorius and Paulinus had already acted upon, without thinking that the gift of the pall was needed for its accomplishment. In his letter to Edwin, the Roman Bishop recommends him to the study of the works of Gregory.

In 630, while Paulinus was still in the north, Eadbald founded a monastery at Dover. Beyond doubt the Monastery of SS. Peter and Paul, at

Canterbury, supplied the nucleus of the new community, which probably, according to the custom of the Middle Ages, consisted of an abbot and twelve brethren; and though the abbot might be one of the Italians, the remainder or the majority of them would, in all likelihood, be Kentish men. We may take this swarm as an evidence that the parent hive was getting overcrowded, and therefore as proof of the continued growth of the Church in Kent.

In the same year an important event had taken place outside the Kingdom of Kent. Sigebert of East Anglia had returned from exile in Burgundy, to succeed to his brother's throne. During his exile he had become a Christian. Bede calls him a most Christian and learned man, and he was desirous of introducing among his people the institutions which he had seen at work in Gaul. It would appear that his wishes had become known to Honorius; very possibly he had sent to Kent to ask for missioners. Just at that time, Felix, a Burgundian, arrived in Canterbury, seeking some field for missionary enterprise, and Honorius sent him into East Anglia. We conclude, from the way in which Bede speaks of him, that he was already a bishop when he came. He established his See at Dunwich, among the south folk. Shortly after, Fursey, an Irish monk, with four companions, came to East Anglia and founded a monastery at Cnobbesburg (Burgh Castle), among the north folk; from these two centres the gospel gradually spread over that kingdom.

CHAPTER XXV

THE KENTISH MONASTERIES

THE episcopate of Honorius witnessed an interesting and important development of the life of the Kentish Church, in the foundation of religious houses for women. Many English ladies of royal and noble birth, in the early times of the conversion, under the teaching and influence of their monkish guides, manifested a strong predilection for the celibate life.

When there were no nunneries in England, they resorted to French religious houses, especially to those at Brie, Chelles, and Andelys; and many of the girls of royal and noble families seem to have been sent thither for their education.

Brie and Chelles were in the neighbourhood of Paris, Andelys was near Rouen. These were all "double" houses, that is, they consisted of two communities, one of monks the other of nuns, in neighbouring buildings, worshipping in one church, all under the rule of an abbess.

About 630, King Eadbald founded at Folkestone a double monastery, after the pattern of these French houses, for his daughter Eanswitha, who became its first abbess. It was the first nunnery in England.

When Ethelburga arrived a fugitive from Northumberland, the King provided for his widowed sister by the gift of the royal residence and estate at Lyminge; which Ethelburga turned into another of these double monasteries, of which she retained the rule. The domestic buildings were probably of timber, but the church, probably of stone, was planned on so large a scale, that it was only half built at the time of her death, 10th September, 647 A.D., and its completion was abandoned.

When Oswald, of the rival royal house of Northumbria, defeated Cædwalla, and mounted the throne in 635 A.D., Ethelburga, fearing that he might seek to extinguish the claims of Edwin's heir by his death, sent the boy Yffi, the son of Osfrith, together with her own boy Wuscfrea, to France, to the care of her uncle, King Dagobert; there both the children died in infancy. Her daughter Eanflæda was brought up in the nunnery at Lyminge; and at length the rivalry between the two houses was reconciled by the marriage of Eanflæda to Oswy, the younger brother and successor of Oswald. Once more we have the incident of a royal bride going from Kent to Northumbria, under the care of the priest Romanus as her chaplain; not because Oswy was a pagan, for he was a saintly Christian man, not necessarily because Oswy was of the Celtic school, though, as a matter of fact, Romanus maintained the Kentish customs in the Queen's household, but because, as has been before explained, it belonged to the dignity of a Queen to have her own chaplain.

The Kentish Church, disheartened perhaps by repeated failures, seems to have abandoned the attempt to plant churches in the other kingdoms, and to have limited its labours to its own people.

We shall shortly find reason to think that it found occupation enough within those limits, and had not men to spare of the character required for foreign adventures. But the Church was being rapidly planted in the other kingdoms by other agencies.

It is not within the scope of the present volume to enter into the details of the conversion of the other kingdoms, but, standing in Kent, the news comes to us of King Oswald's invitation to the fathers of Iona to undertake the evangelisation of Northumbria, and the mission of Aidan in 635; of the coming of the Italian Birinus to the West Saxons; and of the baptism of King Cynegils in the following year.

In 640 A.D., King Eadbald died, and was succeeded by his son Earconbert. He had two sons, Eormenred and Earconbert; why the eldest son did not succeed his father we are not told; the natural conjecture is that he died before him; but he was married and left a daughter, who founded a double monastery (minster) in the Isle of Thanet, and her daughter, St. Mildred, abbess of the monastery, became one of the popular saints of the Kentish Church.

The new King married Sexburh, daughter of Anna, King of the East Angles, a family illustrious in the annals of the Church. For King Anna had four daughters, this Sexburh, who founded a minster in the Isle of Sheppey, and retired to it on her widowhood; Etheldreda, who founded Ely; Ethelberga, who retired to the Monastery of Brie and became its abbess; and Withberga, who passed her life in religious retirement at East Deorham, in her own country. Nor were these all who deserve mention here. Ethelhere, who succeeded his brother Anna on the throne, had married another devout princess, Hereswith, of the family of Edwin of Northumbria, who ended her life as a nun at Chelles; and Hilda, her sister, was the famous Abbess of Whitby. King Aldwulf, the son of Ethelhere and Hereswith, had three daughters: Eadburh became Abbess of Repton, and Ethelburga and Hwælburga successively Abbesses of Hackness. The daughter of Earconbert and Sexburh was also a nun at Brie, and had a great reputation for holiness.

Of King Earconbert we are told that he was the first of the English kings who, by his supreme authority, commanded that the idols throughout his whole kingdom should be forsaken and destroyed; and that the fast of forty days before Easter should be observed; and appointed proper and suitable punishments for the offenders against these laws. The first of these edicts reveals the fact that the old religion, its idols and its worship, still lingered in Kent forty years after the conversion; but that the general sentiment of the people was against the adherents of the old paganism.

Four years (644 A.D.) after the accession of Earconbert, Paulinus died, after nineteen years' occupation of the See of Rochester. When we call to mind that it is now nearly half a century since the band of Italian missionaries set out from their monastery, we recognise that the elders of the band must before this have been lying in the cloisters of Christ Church or of St. Augustine's, in their last sleep, and that the youngest of them must have become old men. Honorius was probably one of the youngest of the band, and one of its last survivors. But there were Kentish men who had been educated in the schools of Canterbury, of whom some had been trained at Christ Church to be priests, and others had joined the monastic community of SS. Peter and Paul, and still others had been drafted off to the new establishments at Dover, Folkestone, and Lyminge.

In the year 653, two young Northumbrians of noble birth, and destined to a great future, spent some time in Kent. Wilfrid came with letters of commendation from Queen Eanflæda to her brother, King Earconbert, desirous of finding an opportunity of going to Rome, and remained about a year. Under what auspices Benedict Biscop came we do not know, but he also was bound for Rome; the two young men set out from Kent in the following year. Wilfrid was afterwards Bishop of York, and Benedict the founder of the Monasteries of Wearmouth and Jarrow.

It is a striking evidence of the fine natural qualities of the English race at that period, that both here in Canterbury and in northern Lindisfarne, in the very first generation of their conversion, the pupils of the Italian and Celtic teachers were, by learning and character, qualified to fill the highest dignities of the Church.

Ithamar, a man of Kentish race, was chosen to succeed Paulinus at Rochester, and was the first Englishman who was consecrated (by Honorius) to be a bishop (644 A.D.); and Bede bears testimony to him that "he was not inferior to his predecessors for learning and conduct of life."

Honorius lived just long enough to hear of the planting of the Church (in 653 A.D.) in two other of the English kingdoms, Mercia and Essex; and while he rejoiced at the extension of Christ's kingdom, it could hardly have been without a feeling of regret that the honour had fallen to the Celtic Church of Northumbria and not to his own countrymen. Peada, the son of the fierce old heathen Penda, King of Mercia, who was now sub-King of the Middle Angles, went to the court of Oswy of Northumbria, to ask his daughter Ethelfleda in marriage. The two families were already allied, for King Oswy's son Alfred was married to Cyneberga, the daughter of King Penda, and sister of Peada. Again we have a repetition of the familiar story, that the Christian house of Northumbria objected to give its daughter in marriage to a heathen. Peada gave a ready ear to the Christian teachers, and "when he heard the preaching of the truth, the promise of the heavenly kingdom, and the hope of resurrection and immortality, he declared that he would willingly become a Christian, even though he should be refused the princess. So he was baptized, with all his earls and soldiers and their servants, who had come with him"; and on his return he took back Chadd and three other English priests, who established the faith among the subjects of Peada.

In the same year, Sigebert, King of the East Saxons, had paid a visit to the court of Oswy, and, chiefly by the reasonings of Oswy on the folly of idolatry, Sigebert and those who had come with him to Northumbria were converted and baptized. On his return, he took back Cedd, the brother of the Chadd just mentioned, and another priest, who set up their centres of teaching at Tilaburg (East Tilbury), on the Thames, and at Ythanacester (Bradwell-on-Sea), at the mouth of the river Pant, and thence converted the East Saxons.

Bishop Honorius died in that same year, 654 A.D., and there was a vacancy of eighteen months before the See was filled. We can only conjecture the cause. Had Paulinus been still alive, he would doubtless have stepped into the vacant chair. Romanus the priest was in Northumbria, and could not be taken away from his position beside the Queen; moreover, with the help of James the Deacon, he was doing what would seem, both at Canterbury and at Rome, the important work of representing the Roman traditions in the north. We must suppose that there were none left of the Italian missionaries, or at least none qualified to keep up the succession. It seems likely that King Earconbert and Bishop Ithamar, in their hereditary deference to the mother Church, referred to Rome, perhaps to have a man sent to them, at least for instructions how to proceed; that they were told to choose the worthiest of their native priests, and that Ithamar received authority to consecrate him. He who was chosen was by race a West Saxon, but we assume that he had been educated and ordained in Kent. His name was Frithonas, but had assumed—or perhaps now assumed—the name of Deusdedit, and he was consecrated, the first native Bishop of Canterbury, 26th March, 655 A.D. The importance of the event is self-evident: it was the withdrawal, as no longer needed, of the leading-strings of Rome from the mission it had sent forth sixty years before, and watched over ever since, and the committal of the Church of Kent to its own resources.

We know nothing certain of the details of the nine years of this episcopate; but we gather that Ithamar died early in it, and Deusdedit consecrated Damian to succeed him, by race a South Saxon, a nation not yet converted to the faith, so that we conclude him to have been one of the clergy of the Kentish Church.

In the time of Deusdedit a new minster was founded in the Isle of Thanet. The legend connected with it is that when Earconbert succeeded to the throne of Kent, it was at the expense of the two infant sons of his elder brother Eormenred, and that, to make his seat secure, Thunor, one of his thanes, with his connivance, murdered the hapless children. When Egbert succeeded to the throne, he made atonement for his father's sin to Mildred, the sister of the slain boys, by granting her as much land in Thanet as a hind could run round in a day. Mildred had been sent to Chelles for education; the wicked abbess tried to persecute the princess into marrying one of her relatives; her mother Eormenburga sent ships to bring her home; the stone on which she first stepped in landing at Ebbe's Fleet bore—it was said—the impress of her foot, and in after years an oratory was built over the sacred spot. Mildred founded a convent on the land given her by Egbert, and, as its abbess, ruled a great community of seventy nuns. St. Mildred became the most popular of the female saints of Kent. Her book of the Gospels was a famous relic. It was said that once when a man took a false oath upon it his eyes dropped out; no wonder it was ever after in great request. In after years there was a great dispute between St. Mary's Minster in Thanet and St. Augustine's at Canterbury, as to which had the honour to possess her bones. St. Mildred came of a family of saints. Her elder sister, St. Milburga, founded a monastery at Wenlock, and was its first abbess; her younger sister, St. Milgitha, was a nun at Eastry in Kent.

But if little happened in Kent in the episcopate of Deusdedit, important events happened in the north, which had a considerable influence upon the history of the Church in Kent and in all England.

The difference between the Celtic and the Canterbury customs did not much matter, so long as the Church of Kent followed one and the Church of Northumbria the other; but they did cause practical inconvenience when King Oswy and his men were keeping the great festival of Easter, while Queen Eanflæda and her household were still in the midst of the austerities of Holy Week. It happened that Agilbert, a French bishop, who had been ministering for some years in Wessex, came on a visit to the Northumbrian court, and Wifrid returned from Rome about the same time. Their observations induced Oswy to summon a synod at Hilda's Monastery of Whitby, to consider the question; and there the King determined to adopt the customs which he was assured were universal in Western Christendom (664). Cedd, Bishop of the East Saxons, was present at the synod, and accepted its decision. Colman, the Bishop of Northumbria, with the Scottish monks and a large company of the English monks of Lindisfarne, refused to abandon the customs of their spiritual forefathers, and retired from the kingdom. Tuda was chosen bishop in Colman's place. Thus the English churches of the Celtic school settled for themselves the question of the customs, not at the demand of Rome, and without even asking Canterbury to assist at the decision.

CHAPTER XXVI

Archbishop Theodore

In the summer of the year 664 A.D. occurred one of those plagues which so frequently ravaged mediæval Europe, it was called the Yellow Pest. In the north the recently-appointed Tuda, Bishop of the Northumbrians, seems to have been one of its victims, and Cedd, Bishop of the East Saxons, died at his Monastery of Lestingay. In the south, Earconbert the King of Kent, and Deusdedit the bishop, died on the same day (July 14), and Damian, Bishop of Rochester, probably died a little before Deusdedit. The plague raged in Essex, and occasioned the sub-King Sigehere, and that part of the people whom he governed, to apostatise from the faith.[1] Egbert succeeded his father on the throne, and the episcopal See remained long vacant. Wilfrid had been chosen to fill Tuda's place in Northumbria, but must needs go to France for consecration, and stay there so long that Chadd was appointed over his head. Chadd came to Kent to seek consecration (664 A.D.), and found when he arrived there that the bishop was dead, and that there was no prospect of a speedy appointment to the vacancy; he therefore went thence to Wini[2] at Winchester,

---
[1] Bede, *Eccl. Hist.* iii. 30.
[2] Wini had been ordained in Gaul.—Bede, *Eccl. Hist.* iii. 7.

who consecrated him, with the assistance of "two bishops of the British nation,[1] who kept Easter after the canonical manner, for at that time there was no other bishop in all Britain canonically ordained besides this Wini." When Wilfrid came back and found his See occupied, Egbert invited him to Kent to do what was required as bishop there during the vacancy.

The affairs of the Church were in confusion; with a double appointment in Northumbria, no bishop at all in Kent, and the East Saxon See vacant; with the Celtic customs still authorised in Mercia, and lingering in Northumbria and Essex, and the South Saxons still unconverted. The Kings of Northumbria and Kent seem to have consulted together on the unsatisfactory state of things. We may with probability credit the older and more experienced, as well as the more powerful, Oswy with the proposal that they should seek the consent of the other kings and churches to choose a man who would be acceptable to all, and send him to Rome to be consecrated there, and, on his return, to exercise the authority of an archbishop over all the churches and bring them into harmony. It was an admirable scheme, and, backed by the influence of the Bretwalda, it met with general acceptance. Wigheard, "a good man and fit priest," one of Deusdedit's clergy, apparently not a monk, was chosen, and sent with some companions to Rome. But Rome, half in ruins, and with the Campagna falling out of cultivation, and becoming the breeding-place of malaria, was an unhealthy place, and Wigheard, with almost all his com-

[1] Bede, *Eccl. Hist.* Perhaps the two bishops of independent West Wales (Devonshire and Cornwall).

panions, died there of pestilence before he could be consecrated, and was buried at the Church of the Apostle St. Peter.

We gather from a letter of Vitalian, then Bishop of Rome, to "Oswy, King of the Saxons," that those who sent Wigheard had agreed not to incur the difficulties and delays of choosing another man of their own, but to ask Vitalian to choose a suitable man, and consecrate and send him; and Vitalian says: "We have not been able yet to find, considering the length of the journey, a man, docile and qualified in all respects to be a bishop, according to the tenor of your letters. But as soon as such a proper person shall be found, we will send him well-instructed to your country, that he may, by word of mouth, and by the divine oracles, with the assistance of God, root out all the enemy's tares throughout your island."

The English kings had sent many vessels of gold and silver as presents to the Roman Bishop; he sends back some relics in return, of the blessed Apostles St. Peter and St. Paul, of the holy martyrs Laurentius, John and Paul, Gregory and Pancratius. Some of these relics would have had a special interest for the disciples of the Italian missionaries in Kent; we have seen that they dedicated one of their churches in Canterbury to St. Pancras and for what reason, the Church of SS. John and Paul, built over the place of their martyrdom, was also on the Cælian Hill. Vitalian possibly supposes that the Northumbrians have inherited the traditions of Canterbury. The Bishop also sends a present to the Queen, a cross, with a gold key, made out of the chains of St. Peter and St. Paul—that is to say, the key had some particles of the chains incorporated into it.

Vitalian made diligent inquiry for some one to send to be Archbishop of the English churches, and did not find one without some trouble. The first man whom he fixed upon was Hadrian, Abbot of the Niridian Monastery, not far from Naples, an African by nation, well versed in Holy Scripture, experienced in ecclesiastical and monastic discipline, and excellently skilled both in the Greek and Latin tongues. Vitalian sent for him, and bade him accept the episcopate and go to Britain. Hadrian, however, excused himself, as being unworthy of so great a dignity, and suggested another, whose age and learning were fitter for the episcopal office, from which we infer that Hadrian was comparatively a young man. The substitute whom he named was a monk named Andrew, belonging to a neighbouring monastery of virgins. He was judged worthy of a bishopric by all who knew him, but bodily infirmity made him unequal to the hardships of the journey to Britain and the labours of the work there. Then Vitalian fell back upon Hadrian, who again asked time to find a substitute.

There was at that time in Rome a monk called Theodore, a native of St. Paul's birthplace, Tarsus in Cilicia. He had lately come to Rome in the train of the Emperor Constans II., whose orthodoxy was very doubtful, and his tyranny beyond all doubt. Theodore was a man of learning in both secular and divine literature, and in both the Greek and Latin languages; of known probity of life, and venerable for his age, for he was sixty-six years old. Hadrian knew him well, and proposed him to Vitalian for the English bishopric. But Vitalian hesitated. Greek ecclesiastics were not in favour at Rome; and one who had been in the train of the Emperor was specially open to suspicion.

Hadrian answered for him, and Vitalian finally agreed to accept him, on condition that Hadrian would accompany him with some of his monks, and take care that he did not, "according to the custom of the Greeks," introduce into the Church over which he presided anything contrary to the true faith.

Theodore turned out to be a man of great energy, sound judgment, and firm will. He united the English churches into a province, over which he ruled as Metropolitan (in all) for one and twenty years.

With Theodore begins a new era in the history of the Church of England, and the history of the Italian mission reaches its conclusion.

Such is the STORY OF AUGUSTINE AND THE ITALIAN MISSION. When we look back upon it, and try to grasp it as a whole, and to estimate the men and their work, we are driven to some judgments which we shrink from pronouncing. Gregory's enterprise was a noble one, undertaken in the sincerest spirit of zeal for the cause of Christ, and of philanthropic interest in the welfare of an interesting people. It was planned on a grand scale, for Gregory sent the flower of his own cherished convent, at his own cost, on this crusade, and the result of the work was fairly satisfactory for a time, and that time is very clearly defined. The events which followed immediately upon Ethelbert's death reveal, beyond the possibility of mistake, that much of the previous success had been due to the influence of Ethelbert, rather than to the initiative of Augustine. It was Ethelbert's diplomacy which obtained the interview between Augustine and the British bishops; the British bishops were not indisposed to welcome a renewal of relations with the Church of Western Christendom, and even to accept Augustine as the link of the new relation; and it was Augustine's fault that the hopeful negotiation failed. It was Ethelbert's political influence which secured the establishment of new centres at Rochester and London; but, on the cessation of that political support, the Bishops of Rochester and London had not obtained sufficient influence to secure even the toleration of their own presence. Even in Kent, the death of Ethelbert was followed by a reaction against Christianity so formidable, that Laurentius contemplated the abandonment of his post.

The impression left on the mind by a consideration of his share in the history is, that Augustine was a pious, good man, possessed with a strong feeling of affectionate and reverent loyalty to his illustrious Abbot and Bishop; and that Gregory had found in him a prior on whom he could entirely rely to maintain the daily routine and discipline of the convent, and to carry out his own directions; but we are driven to the conclusion that the capable and trustworthy lieutenant did not possess the self-reliance, force of character, constructive power, and influence over other men, which make a great leader.

Every man is not a born genius—not to go beyond the scope of the present history—like Gregory or like Theodore; all that the rest of us can do is to give our best to God, as Augustine seems to have done. He had weaknesses and made mistakes—who is free from them? After all, he was the first to preach the gospel to the English; and the results of his work have lived to this day, and will live; and his name will be held in deserved honour so long as the history of the English race shall last.

After the death of Ethelbert, there is no indication of any further attempt to extend the gospel into the other English kingdoms—the mission of Paulinus to Northumbria in the suite of Ethelburga was hardly an exception. All the later bishops seem to have abandoned the hope of carrying out Gregory's great plans for the evangelisation and the ecclesiastical organisation of the English, and to have resigned themselves to the position of Bishops of Kent.

When we consider the relations between Rome and the English mission, we seem to see that Augustine and his successors of the Italian line regarded their Church as holding a position of special dependence upon Rome; they kept up an occasional correspondence with Rome, and sought the advice and sanction of its Bishop at special crises. On the other hand, after the death of Gregory, the mission was not very earnestly backed up from Rome. Its Bishops accepted the deference paid to them; they did what was asked of them, which was usually to give their sanction to some foregone conclusion about the succession or consecration of the English bishops; and they took these opportunities to send complimentary letters to princes and bishops. But they left the mission entirely to its own resources — with the solitary exception that, when Birinus was seeking a sphere of missionary work, Honorius recommended him to go to Britain, and preach in some part of it yet untouched.

In fine, the work of the Italian mission survived in Kent only; we may include Ithamar, Damian, and Deusdedit as belonging to it. With the death of Deusdedit, the Italian succession comes to an end. The consecration of Theodore, with the consent of all the princes and churches of the Heptarchy, is the beginning of a new era. He united all the Heptarchic Churches into one ecclesiastical province, with Canterbury for its Metropolis; he was the first Archbishop of Canterbury, for Bede is witness that he was "the first Archbishop whom all the English Church obeyed."[1]

[1] Bede, *Eccl. Hist.* iv. 2.

INDEX

ALARIC, his sack of Rome, 2
Aquileia, not in communion with Rome for 150 years, 6
Augustine, Prior of St. Andrew's, 19; sent on the English mission, 19; returns from Marseilles, 29; fresh start, with authority as abbot, 21; journey through France, 33–40; received by Ethelbert, 47; enters Canterbury, 48; restores Christ Church, 79; his miracles, 101; founds the Monastery of SS. Peter and Paul, 117; negotiates with the British bishops, 126; extends the Church to Rochester and London, 152; consecrates Laurentius as his successor, 153; his death, 153; his character, 201
"Augustine's Oak," synod at, 131, 140

BANGOR, British monastery at, 144
Belisarius, his re-conquest of Italy, 3
Benedict Biscop, 191
Bertha, Queen, 46, 62
——, Gregory's letters to, 63
Bishops, position of, under the Barbarian conquerors of the Empire, 9
—— of Rome, their position in the sixth and seventh centuries, 11
Books brought by Augustine and sent to him by Gregory, 107

Bretwalda, meaning of, 43
Brunhilda, Queen, Gregory's letters to, 35, 91

CÆDWALLA defeats Edwin and conquers Northumbria, 182
Candidus, agent of the patrimony at Marseilles, 17, 26, 34
Celtic Church customs, 132–137
Christ Church, Canterbury, 79–83
Church of the Four Crowned Martyrs at Canterbury, 161
Churches of the Roman Britons in Kent, 56, 79, 114–116
Columbanus, 155
Crypts of Christ Church, Canterbury, Ripon, and Hexham, 82

DAMIAN, Bishop of Rochester, 193
Deusdedit, Bishop of Canterbury, 193; his death, 196
"Dooms" of Ethelbert, 125

EADBALD, King of Kent, opposes Laurentius, 158; his conversion, 160; founds Church of St. Mary, 162; founds monastery at Dover, 185; at Folkestone, 187; his death, 189
Eanflæda, 172
Earconbert, King of Kent, 189; puts down the old idolatry, 190; his death, 196
Ebbe's Fleet, 39
Edwin, King of Northumbria, his history, 169, 181; conversion,

INDEX

175; power and state, 181; death, 182
Egbert, King of Kent, 196
Ethelbert of Kent, 44; receives Augustine in Thanet, 46, 54; Gregory's letter to, 103; his second marriage, 158; his death, 157; his character, 157
Ethelburga married to Edwin, King of Northumbria, 163; Boniface's letter to her, 165; returns to Kent, 183

FELIX, the Burgundian, first Bishop of East Anglia, 186
Forum, story of the English slave children in, 15

GENSERIC, his sack of Rome, 2
Gregory the Great, his parentage, 7; prætor of Rome, 7; built monastery in Rome, 7; sent as the bishop's agent to Constantinople, 8; elected bishop, 11; his character, 12; writings, 12; likeness, 13; interview with the English slave children in the Forum, 16; starts on a mission to England, 17; compelled to return, 17; sends Augustine and his monks, 19; his letters, 20, 30, 33-38; to Augustine, 66-75

HONORIUS, one of the boy-pupils of Gregory, consecrated at Lincoln as Bishop of Canterbury, 179; his death, 193

ITHAMAR succeeds Paulinus at Rochester, 191

JAMES the Deacon, 164, 183
Justus sent to England, 87; consecrated Bishop of Rochester, 147; flees to the Continent, 159; succeeds Mellitus at Canterbury, 162; receives the pall, 162

KENT, kingdom of, 41, 50-54

LAURENTIUS the Priest, accompanies Augustine to England, 32; sent with letters to Gregory, 61, 63; sent again to Rome, 87; consecrated Bishop of Canterbury, 153; his letter to the bishops of Ireland, 154; and of Britain, 156; about to flee from Kent, 159; his death, 161
Liudhard, Bishop, 46, 72
Lombards, their conquests in Italy, 3
London, foundation of the See at, 147

MELLITUS, Abbot, sent by Gregory to England, 87; consecrated Bishop of the East Saxons, 147; sent to Rome, 156; flees to the Continent, 159; returns to Canterbury, 160; succeeds Laurentius there, 161; his death, 162
Mildred, Abbess, 194
Minster in Thanet, foundation of, 194
—— Sheppey, foundation of, 189
Miracles of Augustine, 101, 138; Gregory's letter on them, 101
Monastery, British, at Bangor, 144
Monastery of SS. Peter and Paul, 117-123
Monasteries in Kent—St. Augustine's, Canterbury, 117; Dover, 185; Folkestone, 187; Lyminge, 188; Minster in Sheppey, 189; Minster in Thanet, 194

NORTHUMBRIA, its condition, 163; Paulinus's mission to, 163; meeting of the Witan, 173

PALL, the, granted to Augustine, 91; history of, 94-100
Patrician, meaning of the title, 36
Paulinus sent to England, 87; consecrated bishop and sent to Northumbria, 164; converts King Edwin, 175; his missionary

work, 177 ; builds churches at Doncaster and Lincoln, 178 ; work at Southwell, 180 ; his personal appearance, 180 ; flight to Canterbury, 183 ; receives the pall, 185 ; succeeds Romanus at Rochester, 184 ; his death, 190

REDWALD, King of the East Angles, converted, 150
Ricimer, his plunder of Rome, 3
Rochester, foundation of the See of, 147
Romanus, consecrated Bishop of Rochester, 162 ; drowned on a voyage to Rome, 184
Rome, condition of, in the sixth century, 4
——, Bishops of, obtain independent sovereignty, 3
——, Church of, its condition in the sixth century, 3
Royal abbesses and nuns, 187, 189
Rufinianus sent to England, 87
Rutupiæ, 39

SEBERT, King of the East Saxons, 148
Sigebert, King of East Anglia, introduces the Church there, 186
Stephen, Abbot of Lerins, 33
St. Martin's Church, Canterbury, 56
Syagrius, Bishop of Autun, 38, 75

TEMPLES, heathen, in Kent, 77, 111-113
Theodebert of Austrasia, Gregory's letters to, 34
Theodore, Archbishop, 199
Theodoric, his conquest of Italy, 3
—— of Austrasia, Gregory's letter to, 34-40

VIRGILIUS of Arles, Gregory's letters to, 22, 74

WILFRID of York, 191

YORK MINSTER, 175

www.ingramcontent.com/pod-product-compliance
Lightning Source LLC
Chambersburg PA
CBHW031832230426
43669CB00009B/1323